The
MIRACLES
of the Messiah

the MIRACLES *of the Messiah*

The Evidence Provided to Attest Jesus was the Christ

Bryan W Sheldon

GOSPEL FOLIO PRESS
www.gospelfolio.com

MIRACLES OF THE MESSIAH
By Bryan W. Sheldon
Copyright © 2006
All rights reserved

Published by
GOSPEL FOLIO PRESS
304 Killaly Street West
Port Colborne, ON, Canada L3K 6A6
1-800-952-2382
www.gospelfolio.com

ISBN 1-897117-39-6

Cover design by Rachel Brooks

Printed in the United States of America.

Contents

Appreciation...7

Prologue...9

Chapter 1
When God Sent His Son 11

Chapter 2
What Claims Did Jesus of Nazareth Make?.....................23

Chapter 3
What Evidence was the Messiah Expected to
Provide to Support His Claim? 33

Chapter 4
Authenticating Miracles in the Synoptic Gospels...........45

Chapter 5
Authenticating Miracles in John's Gospel:
Introduction...59

Chapter 6
Authenticating Miracles in John's Gospel:
The Attesting Signs..69

Chapter 7
How Did the Nation's Leaders Investigate His
Claims? 95

Chapter 8
What was the Decision of the Nation's Leaders? 113

Chapter 9
What was the Response of Jesus to Their Decision? 117

Chapter 10
The Sign of the Prophet Jonah 131

Chapter 11
A Final Summary...159

Bibliography...163

Appreciations

Let me publicly acknowledge the debt I owe to the late, great, Ieuan Jones, Bible teacher extraordinaire.

Let me also acknowledge my indebtedness to those fine Christian writers whose work lives on: from Lightfoot, through Edersheim, to the current generation of teachers like Fruchtenbaum. May the Lord continue to bless their teaching.

My thanks also to Isobel, Rachel and Ron for their help and encouragement.

Prologue

Why did the Sanhedrin, the religious rulers of Israel, reject the Messianic claims of Jesus[1] of Nazareth? Did He not have the right credentials? Did He not perform the correct, authenticating miracles? Did they consider Him an impostor? Were there perhaps other political expediencies dictating their actions? Was their decision a proper, considered judgment, or were they already predisposed to reject the claim of any individual who wished to change the status quo? This book examines the New Testament record and scrutinizes the conflict between Jesus of Nazareth and the Sanhedrin, since the consequences of that decision, by a relatively small group of Jewish leaders, has affected all humankind for nearly two millennia.

At the heart of the conflict was the matter of the miracles of the Messiah. They will be set in the context of the Jewish culture of the day, and their significance will be weighed.

---

1   In view of the fact that this small volume deals with the Jewish setting of the Messianic claims of Jesus, His Hebrew name, i.e. "Yeshua" was considered for use in the text. However, since all New Testament quotes use the name 'Jesus' we will follow this practice.

Chapter 1
When God Sent His Son

The Condition of the Jewish Nation at the Time of the Incarnation

Writers of the T'nach, the Jewish Scriptures, prophesied the coming of a deliverer; an anointed one; a Messiah; an individual who would be of the seed of woman, and descended from Abraham, Isaac, Jacob, Judah and David. Moses said he would be an anointed prophet (Deut. 18:15); David said he would be a priest of the order of Melchizedek (Ps. 110:4); Micah said he would rule Israel (Mic. 5:2). Jesus of Nazareth claimed to be that Messiah. Moreover, beyond His work as Messiah, He claimed to be God incarnate, deity clothed in flesh. Evidence in support of these claims was mostly in the area of the miraculous.

At the time of His unveiling, Israel was in captivity, both nationally and spiritually. The land, promised to Abraham and his seed, was enemy-held territory.

The Political Climate

Rome/Pilate

The standards, symbols and activities of Rome, the unlawful occupants, were everywhere. The Jewish Temple, for all its great height, was itself overlooked by the towers of the Antonia fortress. This physically illustrated the plight of the nation. The Antonia fortress was a monstrosity which housed the Roman garrison. It abutted the Herodian extensions of the Temple at the north-western corner of the Temple mount. The physical might of the Roman army enforced the payment of taxes levied on the Jewish people, and compelled their obedience to Roman law. Jesus alludes to the subservience of Jewish citizens to Roman citizens in the Sermon on the Mount when He said, *"Whoever compels you to go one mile..."* (Matt. 5:41).

At the time of the ministry and death of Christ, Pilate was the occupying forces' highest authority in Israel. He was in charge of as many as 5,000 infantry, stationed in Caesarea and Jerusalem, as well as approximately 120 cavalry. He appointed the High Priests and controlled the Temple and its funds. The High Priest's vestments were in Pilate's keeping and he only released them for festivals, at which time he reinforced the garrison in Jerusalem.

The Herods

Under Rome, there was a period when the secular rulers of Israel were the Herods. There are seven of them mentioned in the New Testament. The first was Herod the Great, the king of the nation at the time of the birth of Jesus. He was not of David's line, nor even of Jacob's line, and therefore not of "Israel". Rather, he was an Idumean, a descendent of Esau, and a Jewish proselyte. Under Rome, he ruled an area the size of which rivalled that of Solomon's kingdom. He thought of himself as a new Solomon, rebuilding the Temple while overcoming all obstacles. He obtained the title, "King of the Jews" and some of the Herodian party considered him a Messiah. However, he was evil, a murderer. To gain power he murdered his masters and those of the Sanhedrin who opposed him. When in power, motivated by jealousy, he murdered Hyrcanus, the grandfather of his favourite wife Mariamne. Then he murdered Mariamne herself, despite being passionately attached to her. He also murdered her two sons, Alexander and Aristobulus, and, only five days before his own death, he killed his own son, Antipater. Furthermore, in his last moments, he gave orders for the execution of a number of his nobles, so that at his death universal mourning might shroud the land. Against this backdrop, his infamous act of massacring the innocents of Bethlehem, was chillingly not out of character. In his will, he bequeathed the kingdom to three of his sons, Archelaus, Antipas and Philip.

It was fear of Archelaus, also a wicked king, which caused Joseph and Mary to take Jesus and settle out of his jurisdiction in Galilee (Matt. 2:22). Because of his repressive rule, the Jews went to Rome to have him deposed. From this time on, procurators[2] governed Judea.

Herod Antipas, a son of Herod the Great by his Samaritan wife Malthace, was tetrarch of Galilee and Peraea during the whole period of the Messiah's life on earth (Luke 23:7). A frivolous and vain prince, he was chargeable with many infamous crimes (Mark 8:15; Luke 3:19; 13:31). He was the one who imprisoned and executed the Messiah's forerunner, John, at the instigation of Herodias, his half-brother Herod-Philip's wife, whom he had married (Matt. 14:1-12). He had a brief encounter with Jesus (Luke 23:7 ff), and was denounced as a plotter by Herod Agrippa (the grandson of Herod the Great). He was deposed, and spent the rest of his life in exile.

Herod Philip I, was the son of Herod the Great by Mariamne, the daughter of Simon, the High Priest. He lived in Rome with his wife Herodias and his daughter Salome. This is the Philip mentioned in Mark 6:17.

Herod Philip II, the son of Herod the Great and Cleopatra of Jerusalem, was tetrarch of Batanea, Iturea, Trachonitis, and Auranitis. He rebuilt the city of Caesarea Philippi, calling it by his own name to distinguish it from the Caesarea on the seacoast, which was the seat of the Roman government. He married Salome, the daughter of Herodias. This is the Philip mentioned in Luke 3:1.

Herod Agrippa ruled over an area as great as his grandfather's kingdom and was known for his attack on the apostles (Acts 12:2). Luke recorded his sudden death in Acts 12:20-23.

These Herods, who under Rome carried the sceptre of law for Israel during the period of the incarnation and the first years of the early church, all proved themselves enemies of what was right and good, and enemies of God's Messiah and His disciples. Israel was not safe while Rome and the Herods remained the major political players.

---

2 Personal agents of the Emperor.

The Spiritual Climate

More serious than Israel's political state was its spiritual state.

Priests and Sadducees

During the ministry of Jesus, a corrupt priesthood ran the Temple. The man who held the greatest authority was Annas, a High Priest who had been deposed by Rome, but who retained power by controlling whoever was the titular High Priest. Caiaphas, his son-in-law, was the High Priest. He officiated at the trials of Jesus and so manipulated events that a guilty verdict was pronounced on an innocent man.

The commercial enterprises of the priesthood exposed their corruption. On the Temple Mount, items essential for ritual offerings were sold at exorbitant prices. The great religious festivals, when Jerusalem was filled with pilgrims from other parts of the Roman Empire as well as the faithful from all over Israel, were used to collect vast amounts of money. For example, the annual Temple-tribute was collected at the season of Passover when the nation's population was greatly increased with pilgrims. Prior to the influx of pilgrims arriving in Jerusalem, the tax gatherers gave their attention to the resident population. A month before 14th Nissan, on 15th Adar, stalls of money-changers were opened in every town in Israel. All Jews and proselytes (except women, slaves and children) were liable for the tax. The Temple-tribute had to be paid in exact half shekels of the Sanctuary. Since the coins in circulation were Persian, Tyrean, Syrian, Egyptian, Roman, Grecian and Galilean, just imagine how much trade these money changers had. Those who did not pay the tribute could have their goods confiscated. These Temple tax collectors were permitted to charge a fee for their services. However, if an individual did not have the right money to pay for the tribute, the money-changer would charge a second fee for providing change. The revenue extracted by these tax collectors/money changers was immense.

On the 25th Adar they moved their stalls to Jerusalem. Then the first pilgrims would be arriving for the feast, and the Temple tax collectors set up in the Temple precincts. They exacted the tribute money from all visitors and charged each their additional fee. Pilgrims visiting from other nations took the opportunity to change their coin into Temple currency, not only to pay the tribute, but also to obtain currency to purchase things needful for the feast, i.e. sacrifices and offerings. These ancient *"bureaux de change"*, set their own exchange rates. The Temple, controlled by Annas and Caiaphas, profited greatly from this trade.

The dealings of these servants of mammon (Matt. 6:24) and Annas involved the weighing of coins, with deductions for the loss of weight, and the subsequent arguments and disputes. It is not unreasonable to suggest that in such circumstances some of these money changers would resort to false and deceptive balances (Amos 8:5; Mic. 6:11). There was cheating, lying and sometimes violence. When Jesus Himself called them *"a den of thieves"* in Matthew 21:13, He had Himself weighed them in a balance and found them wanting (Dan. 5:27).

Since these people were in a close business relationship with Annas and Caiaphas, they were examples of the character of the leaders of the nation, which is borne out by the fact that the Messiah used the same word of Annas, Caiaphas and the Chief Priests as He did of these corrupt financiers. *"All who came before Me are thieves and robbers, but the sheep did not hear them"* (John 10:8).[3] The Sadducean High Priest, who should have been a shepherd to Israel, was branded by the Messiah as a thief. The Temple "market", in Rabbinical writings, is referred to as "the Bazaars of the Sons of Annas" (*Chanuyoth beney Chanan*). The priests were running a monopoly and worshippers were fleeced like the sheep they sacrificed! Edersheim quotes Josephus and other sources where Annas is described as "a great hoarder up of money, very rich".[4] He despoiled the common priests of their official revenues. The Talmud records the curse that a Rabbi of Jerusalem (Rabbi Abba Shaul) pronounced on the High Priestly families (including that of Annas) who were "High Priests and their sons were [Temple] treasurers and their sons-in-law assistant treasurers and their servants beat the people with staves."[5]

---

3   see also Matt. 6:19.
4   Alfred Edersheim, Life & Times of Jesus the Messiah (Peabody: hendrickson Publishers Inc., 2000) Book 3, p. 256.
5   Pesahim 57a (Babylonian Talmud).

There were 24 groups or courses of priests officiating in the Temple (1 Chron. 23:6); a chief priest at the head of each. Most of the priests were Sadducees. According to early Christian writers (Hippolytus, Origen, and Jerome), the Sadducees accepted only the first five books of the T'nach (the Pentateuch) as inspired text. The remainder of the T'nach (the Prophets and the Writings), while not rejected outright, were considered redundant for doctrinal purposes. For example, they did not believe in a resurrection since it was not in the Pentateuch (Luke 20:27; cf. Acts 4:1,2; 23:6-8). This is why Jesus took His proof text from the most well known passage in the Pentateuch to confound them on the subject (Mark 12:26; Luke 20:37). Josephus asserted their rejection of "the immortal duration of the soul, and the punishments and rewards in Hades."[6] "Souls die with the bodies" was what they believed.[7] The practical effect of this doctrine was to "eat, drink and be merry, for tomorrow we die." They were called the Epicureans of the Jews. Since their theological position did not include reward or retribution after death, they were left with no restraint in the present.

The Pharisees

The priests exercised a great deal of power through the Sanhedrin, the highest court in Israel, where they held 24 of the 70 seats. The High Priest occupied an extra seat, reserved for the leader of the court. Alongside the priests in the Sanhedrin were elders and leaders of Israel who largely held to the doctrine of the Pharisees. These considered themselves the descendents of Ezra, the father of Jewish legalism and of the Hasidim, who had so heroically resisted the Hellenisation of the Jews. The Hasidim were those Jews who had resisted to the death the attacks on the Jewishness of the Hebrew nation by Antiochus Epiphanes and the Seleucids. This history had left its mark, so they defended with vigour any weakening of their traditional position.

The Pharisees, in contrast to the Sadducees, accepted the whole of the T'nach (the Law, the Writings and the Prophets); and added other regulations which they sought to impose on the population. These other laws and regulations were called

6   The Wars of the Jew 2.8.14 (The Works of Josephus).
7   The Antiquities of the Jews 18.1.4 (The Works of Josephus).

the "tradition of the elders"; and revolved around the practical application of the T'nach. The Pharisees worked hand in hand with the interpreters of these traditions, the Scribes, but Jesus condemned both Scribes and Pharisees for hypocrisy. They pretended spirituality; they pretended integrity; they pretended they were following the light of the Word of God, but Jesus said they were like the Sadducees: corrupt, extortioners, exploiting the people, devouring widows' houses (Mark 12:40; Luke 20:47). Described as blind leaders of the blind, they were a generation of vipers.

Historically, these "rulers of Israel", (Sadducean priests and Pharisaic elders and lawyers), met in the house of polished stones in the Temple compound, but at the time of the ministry of the Messiah they were meeting in the end chambers of the royal porch, located on the southern wall of the Temple mount.[8]

Satan

The population itself was largely in a state of unbelief, and was therefore ripe for the activities of the Adversary. When Jesus began His ministry, one of His first tasks was as a medical missionary to the demon possessed. This condition revealed itself in many ways, with some deaf, some blind, some mute, some paralyzed, some lunatic and some spastic. Many in Israel had been "bound by Satan" for a considerable period. Lightfoot expresses it in his commentary on Matthew 10:

> When I consider with myself that numberless number of demoniacs which the evangelists mention, the like to which no history affords, and the Old Testament produces hardly one or two examples, I cannot but suspect …that the Jewish people, now arriving to the very top of that impiety, now also arrived to the very top of those curses which are recited in Leviticus chapter 26 and Deuteronomy chapter 28.[9]

Then there were those who, while not possessed, were oppressed of the devil. Luke referred to it when he reported, "*Jesus*

---

8   "Trade Halls" — Shabbat 15a (Babylonian Talmud).
9   John Lightfoot, Commentary on New Testament from the Talmud and Hebraica (Peabody: Hendrickson Publishers Inc., 2003) p. 177.

17

of Nazareth…went about doing good and healing all who were oppressed by the devil, for God was with Him" (Acts 10:38). It appears that Jesus first had to cleanse the nation of demonic activity before they could have the freedom to consider His claims of office. Jesus likened the nation to a man possessed of an unclean demon (Matt. 12:43-44).

The gospel writers themselves give eye-witness descriptions of this activity: *"They brought to Him many who were demon-possessed. And He cast out the spirits with a word, and healed all who were sick"* (Matt. 8:16); and, *"He was preaching in their synagogues throughout all Galilee, and casting out demons"* (Mark 1:39). His disciples who joined Him in this ministry said, *"Lord, even the demons are subject to us in Your name"* (Luke 10:17); and they too, *"cast out many demons"* (Mark 6:13). The activity and influence of Satan was so strong at this time that the Messiah made a general statement to say of those who opposed Him that they were children of the devil (John 8:44). Significantly, their retort was that Jesus Himself was demon-possessed, a charge patently untrue and which Jesus denied (John 8:48,52).

Then Israel's Messiah Arrived!

To such a people, oppressed by Rome, in captivity to Satan, and ruled by a corrupt Sanhedrin, God's Messiah came. He was their only hope. He came and offered a kingdom. His message to the nation was, *"the kingdom of heaven is at hand"* (Matt. 4:17), a message previously ministered by His herald, John (Matt. 3:2), and later given to His disciples to preach (Matt. 10:7). What was this kingdom? What exactly was He offering? As Messiah, He offered a kingdom headed by Himself, that is the Messianic kingdom, the kingdom of peace. Great David's greater Son would banish Satan and occupy David's throne. It would be a time of prosperity for all. The animals would be subject to man, as in the garden of Eden and the government at Jerusalem would dispense justice righteously. Truth and holiness would characterize many of its citizens and people would plant, harvest, and build. Righteousness would be the prevailing characteristic of this kingdom (Heb. 1:8). The old order would give way to a new order, "new wine in new bottles".

God gave the nation a choice: to receive or to reject His Deliverer. But, as the ministry of Jesus developed, it became clear that embracing the new order would mean the leadership of the nation would be greatly affected:

(a) The Romans would, of necessity, be compelled to yield the government of Israel. In addition, they would stand trial on charges of anti-Semitism (Matt. 25:31-46).

(b) In a similar manner, Herod would lose both his political power and wealth, and face trial.

(c) The Sadducean leadership would lose their position in the Mosaic hierarchy, and in consequence, lose also their income and their influence over the nation. The fortunes of Annas and Caiaphas would be forfeit.

(d) The Pharisees' place on Israel's stage would be over, since Messiah branded them as hypocrites, and refused to endorse their traditions. They too, would lose their position, power, and source of income.

However, Satan exerted a powerful influence on all levels of society. Ultimately the nation, led by the Sanhedrin, rejected the Messianic claims of Jesus. Since they knew that He was their Messiah, their actions made them culpable. But why did they reject Him? John answered this question. *"This is the condemnation, that the light has come into the world, and men loved darkness rather than light, because their deeds were evil. For everyone practicing evil hates the light and does not come to the light, lest his deeds should be exposed"* (John 3:19-20).

It is not as if the rejection was unexpected by God and His Messiah. While the offer of the Messianic kingdom was genuine, the rejection of the Messiah meant the rejection of the kingdom. The Messianic kingdom would have to be postponed until a generation could be found to call for Jesus Messiah, and to embrace the principles of the kingdom—judgment, mercy and faith (Matt. 23:23). Israel would have to wait for a time when the nation's leadership would call for the return of the Messiah they had previously rejected. Jesus said, *"I say to you, you shall see Me no more till you say, 'Blessed is He who comes in the name of the Lord!'"* (Matt. 23:39).

Was There Any Expectation of a Messiah in the Jewish Nation at the Time of the Incarnation?

Students of the T'nach were familiar with those times when God had provided a prophetic indicator of great deliverances. For example, because of His words to Abraham, Israel might have anticipated a Moses after 400 years in Egypt (Gen. 15:13). Certainly, Daniel was able to mark the end of the Babylonian captivity after 70 years, because of the prophecy of Jeremiah (Dan. 9:2). Therefore, those who pored over the pages of the T'nach at the beginning of the Christian era would have been aware of Daniel's prophecy which spoke of a period of 69 "sevens" of years, that is 483 years, from the edict for the rebuilding of Jerusalem after the Babylonian exile to the coming of *"Messiah the Prince"* (Dan. 9:25). These scholars looked for any indications of the unveiling of the Messiah.

And for those who had eyes to see, there were signs that the time of Messiah had come. There had been that incident when an elderly priest had testified that during the ceremony of the burning of the incense, he had seen an angel in the Temple, who had brought a message of the coming of the Messiah (Luke 1:5 ff). The angel was the very same Gabriel who had been instrumental in giving the timetable of Messiah's coming to Daniel (Dan. 8:16; 9:21; Luke 1:19,26). Events surrounding the angelic visit helped to confirm the veracity of the message. The old priest was struck dumb and a son was miraculously born to the old couple, on whose birth the old priest was able to speak again. Friends and neighbours spread the news throughout Judea (Luke 1:64-65).

Six months after the birth of the son of the priest, the *"light and glory of God"* shone above the hills around Bethlehem (Luke 2:9). This light, the Shekinah of God, had been visible, even in Babylonia, where the eastern stargazers marked it and understood its significance (Matt. 2:2). Temple shepherds, who had witnessed the Shekinah glory, reported further angelic messages of the birth of the Messiah (Luke 2:8 ff).

Then there was the testimony of those who were recognized to be under the inspiration of the Spirit of God. Some six weeks after the shepherds had seen the Shekinah glory of God, the parents of the baby, identified by heaven as the Messiah, went up to the Temple to fulfil their obligations—the offering of sacrifice for the purification of the mother, and the payment of money for the redemption of the first-born. Following the priestly benediction on the infant, a godly man, Simeon, entered the court of prayer, held the child in His arms and declared the baby to be God's Messiah (Luke 2:25-26). This man was not only a student of the Scriptures and therefore aware of the timing of the coming of the Messiah, but also a godly man who had received an indication from God that he would not die until he saw the *"Consolation of Israel"*. The prophetess, Anna, likewise declared Him to be her Messiah (Luke 2:38).

Nearly two years after these events, the eastern stargazers, who had seen from afar the Shekinah glory over the hills of Bethlehem, arrived in Jerusalem on a visit and *"troubled"* both Herod and Jerusalem with the question, *"Where is He who has been born King of the Jews?"* (Matt 2:2). Herod, clearly aware of the Messianic expectations of the nation at that time, called some of the Sanhedrin and asked where the Messiah was to be born (v. 4). They identified Bethlehem, which village suffered a great tragedy some time later when Herodian soldiers slaughtered all of the boys younger than twenty-five months. It was Herod's attempt, no doubt prompted by a higher, evil, power, to kill the young Messiah (vv. 16-18).

As the years passed, anticipation first waned and then increased again when tokens of God's favour occurred. The pool at Bethesda had healing power at certain seasons (John 5:4), and Jewish exorcists were casting out demons (Matt. 12:27). These very significant and unprecedented events were tokens that God was beginning to loosen Satan's grip on the ancient people of God. There was another power at work in Israel. The population of Jerusalem had increased year-by-year, having been led by Daniel's prophecy and the agreeableness of the time to live there, in expectation of the Messiah. Accordingly, many of the people were waiting for the kingdom of God (Luke 19:11), among them some who held eminent positions like Counsellor Joseph of Arimathaea, an honourable man (Mark 15:43). At this time, John, the son of the old priest, Zacharias, began His prophesied ministry. Those who were anticipating the coming of Israel's Deliverer, flocked to hear him and to be baptized (Luke 3:15). Indeed, the question as to whether John was the predicted Messiah was constantly raised (John 1:19; 3:28). Jesus Himself was subjected to the same questioning by those who had been alerted by Daniel's prophecy (John 10:24). The woman at Jacob's well in Samaria voiced precisely the intelligence that was circulating, *"I know that Messiah is coming (who is called Christ)"* (John 4:25).

From such incidents it is concluded that the nation was expecting the unveiling of a national Messiah.

Let us examine the gospel narratives to explore the way Jesus of Nazareth presented Himself to the population and how they reacted to Him. We will identify His claims and His confirming evidence. We will further identify their response and the motives for their actions.

The following questions are phrased to guide our research into the relevant areas, and to be able to assess the relationship of the people of Israel with their Messiah during the period of the incarnation.

What claims did Jesus of Nazareth make? Did He claim to be Israel's Messiah? (chapter 2)

What evidence was the Messiah expected to provide to support his claim? (chapter 3)

What evidence did Jesus of Nazareth provide? (chapters 4-6)

How did the nation's leaders investigate His claims, and what did they decide? (chapters 7-8)

How did Jesus respond to their decision? (chapter 9)

How did it all end? (chapter 10)

Chapter 2

What Claims Did Jesus of Nazareth Make?

Did Jesus of Nazareth Claim to be Israel's Messiah?

Jesus of Nazareth, in addition to the Messianic ministry He pursued, presented a Messianic claim in different ways, at different times. The first time was when He was about thirty years of age. In His home synagogue, He identified Himself as Messiah by reading a Messianic passage from Isaiah 61: *"The Spirit of the Lord is upon Me, Because He has anointed Me to preach the gospel to the poor; He has sent Me to heal the brokenhearted, to proclaim liberty to the captives and recovery of sight to the blind, to set at liberty those who are oppressed; to proclaim the acceptable year of the Lord."* This quote is at the heart of any definition of a Messiah, "an anointed one". Jesus, in saying, *"Today this Scripture is fulfilled in your hearing"* (Luke 4:18-21), claimed *"the Spirit of the Lord is upon Me"* and *"He has anointed Me"*. This essential Messianic qualification had been effected at Jordan when Jesus was baptized, for on that occasion the Spirit of God descended and remained on Him.[10]

Then, in a continuing defence of His Messianic claim over a long period, He spoke repeatedly of *"the Father who sent me"*.[11]

John 5:22-30 records His declaration that He had been sent as God's co-equal to be the Messiah. Therefore, He should be honoured with the same honour that is afforded to God. Furthermore, He has the same power to impart life, as does the

---

10   Matt.3:16; Mark 1.10, Luke 3:22; John 1:32.
11   John 5:23,30,36-37; 6:39,44,57; 8:16,18,29,42; 10:36; 12:49; 14:24.

Father. Those who honour Jesus with the same honour as they give to the Father will be recipients of the life of God. This is the true ministry of the Messiah.

Verses 36 and 37 of the same chapter record Jesus' appeal to His confirming miracles as evidence that He was their Messiah; *"For the works which the Father has given Me to finish—the very works that I do—bear witness of Me, that the Father has sent Me"*.

In His teaching to the crowd that had enjoyed the miraculous provision of bread and fish, He repeated the essence of the truth that there is an unbreakable, invisible, symbiotic connection between Him and His co-equal Father. This truth is incorporated into His mission as the commissioned Messiah from heaven: *"For I have come down from heaven, not to do My own will, but the will of Him who sent Me. This is the will of the Father who sent Me, that of all He has given Me I should lose nothing, but should raise it up at the last day. And this is the will of Him who sent Me, that everyone who sees the Son and believes in Him may have everlasting life; and I will raise him up at the last day* (John 6:38-40). *"No one can come to Me unless the Father who sent Me draws him; and I will raise him up at the last day"* (v. 44). *"As the living Father sent Me, and I live because of the Father, so he who feeds on Me will live because of Me"* (v. 57).

After His rejection, He referred to His disciples as those who knew that God had sent him (John 17:25) and asked that their testimony might confirm the same truth (v. 21).

When speaking to individuals He made clear references to His mission. The woman at Jacob's well said: *"I know that Messiah is coming. When He comes, He will tell us all things"*; to which Jesus replied: *"I who speak to you am He"* (John 4:25-26). This truth was communicated to the people of Samaria, for they said; *"Now we believe, not because of what you said, for we ourselves have heard Him and we know that this is indeed the Messiah, the Saviour of the world"* (John 4:42). He asked a newly healed blind man, *"Do you believe in the Son of God?"* and received the response: *"Who is He, Lord, that I may believe in Him?"* And Jesus said to him: *"You have both seen Him and it is He who is talking with you"* (John 9:35-37).

When John was in prison and needed some assurance that Jesus was indeed the Messiah, he sent some of his disciples to obtain a helpful response from his cousin to ease his troubled mind. Jesus sent back John's messengers with instructions to tell him that the Messianic prophecies of Isaiah were being fulfilled: *"The blind see and the lame walk; the lepers are cleansed and the deaf hear; the dead are raised up and the poor have the gospel preached to them"* (Matt. 11:5).[12]

With respect to His own disciples, Jesus spent no little time educating them until they were clear about His person and mission. When Peter said: *"You are the Messiah, the Son of the living God"* (Matt. 16:16), Jesus commended him in the most fulsome terms.

When His opponents challenged Him: *"How long do You keep us in doubt? If You are the Christ (Messiah), tell us plainly"*, He responded: *"I told you, and you do not believe. The works that I do in My Father's name, they bear witness of Me"* (John 10:24-25).

Did Jesus of Nazareth Claim to be God Incarnate?

Certainly! He implied as much when He said, *"I and My Father are one"* (John 10:30; 5:18 ff). Those who heard Him make this statement understood it as such. They accused Him of blasphemy. The language of the Messiah is the language of the incarnate God, revealed on earth as Son of the Father. Jesus said, *"My Father has been working until now, and I have been working"* (John 5:17). The Bible describes the reaction of the people: *"Therefore the Jews sought all the more to kill Him, because He not only broke the Sabbath, but also said that God was His Father, making Himself equal with God"* (v. 18).

In the "Good Shepherd" discourse, He added some detail to the assertion that He was equal to the Father. Jesus said He could give His sheep eternal life, and that He guaranteed their eternal safety because He, together with His co-equal Father, had the power to keep them secure. *"And I give them eternal life, and they shall never perish; neither shall anyone snatch them out of My hand. My Father, who has given them to Me, is greater than all; and no one is able to snatch them out of My Father's hand"* (John 10:28-29). The eternal keeping power of Jesus is here asserted to be the same as that of the Father. The reaction of the people

---

12   cf. Isa. 32:3; 42:7.

again confirmed their understanding that Jesus was claiming deity. For the Jews took up stones again to stone Him. Jesus challenged this demonstration of anger and hatred: *"Many good works I have shown you from My Father. For which of those works do you stone Me?"* His opponents answered Him, *"For a good work we do not stone You, but for blasphemy, and because You, being a Man, make Yourself God"* (John 10:31-33).

In less hostile surroundings Jesus also confirmed to His disciples that, *"He who has seen Me has seen the Father"* (John 14:9).

When Jesus stood before members of the Sanhedrin, Caiaphas, the High Priest put Him under oath and demanded a direct answer to a direct question. *"I put You under oath by the living God: Tell us if You are the Christ* [Messiah], *the Son of God!"* (Matt. 26:63). This precise question brought into focus the two main elements in the dilemma they faced: what was the nature of the person and work of Jesus of Nazareth? With respect to the mission of Jesus, he asked, *"Are you the Messiah?"* In respect of Christ's personal essence, he asked "Are you the Son of God?" Jesus gave a clear, affirmative answer to both halves of the question, *"It is as you said"* (v. 64). Furthermore, He increased their consternation by quoting a Messianic prophecy from Daniel that supported both the issues under consideration. The Rabbinic interpretation of Daniel 7:13-14 was that the Son of Man named there was both Messiah and divine. Jesus therefore said, *"...hereafter you will see the Son of Man sitting at the right hand of the Power, and coming on the clouds of heaven"* (Matt. 25:64). Jesus claimed that, at a future time, He would return, and according to Daniel 7:14, the Ancient of Days would give Him an everlasting dominion, with glory, and an eternal kingdom. Furthermore, all nations would serve and worship Him. Caiaphas understood the implication of Jesus' words. The High Priest tore his clothes, and declared: *"He has spoken blasphemy! What further need do we have of witnesses? Look, now you have heard His blasphemy!"* (Matt. 26:65). There can be no doubt that Jesus understood Himself to be Son of God in the fullest sense. When the opponents of Jesus had difficulty in supplying evidence to Pilate to support the political charges laid against Him, they fell back on, *"We have a law, and according to our law He ought to die, because He made Himself the*

Son of God" (John 19:7). The law to which they referred was the law of blasphemy.[13]

"Son of God" is, as the High Priest understood it, and John used it, a title of deity. It is also most appropriate when we consider the miraculous circumstances of His birth, for He was conceived of the Holy Spirit (Luke 1:35).

Here are some other key references, to Jesus, the "Son of God":

After the amazing episode when Jesus had walked on water, saved Peter from the deep and calmed the storm, the disciples coupled the use of this title with worship, which for a Jew is reserved solely for God. The disciples, convinced of the deity of their Master, said, *"Truly You are the Son of God"* (Matt. 14:33).

In the great crowd of sick people, those possessed by unclean spirits fell down before Him and acknowledged His deity, saying: *"You are the Son of God"* (Mark 3:11).[14]

The Gadarene demoniac, "Legion", recognized His divine nature and authority when he used the title: *"Jesus, Son of the Most High God"*. The demons who inhabited the demented man, begged the incarnate God, *"not* [to] *command them to go out into the abyss"*, a power only possessed by God (Luke 8:28 ff).

The identifying sign given to the forerunner of the Messiah included the understanding that the one on whom the Spirit of God rested was the One who would immerse His followers in the Holy Spirit. Surely this was an act only available to God, as Isaiah indicated by his rhetorical question, *"Who has directed the Spirit of the Lord* [YHWH]*?"* (Isa. 40:13); a question that demands the answer, "only YHWH". John the Baptist recognized the sign and identified Jesus saying, *"This is the Son of God"* (John 1:34).

Nathanael, impressed by the omniscience displayed by Jesus, declared, *"Rabbi, You are the Son of God! You are the King of Israel!"* (John 1:49).

The healing of the man born blind was sufficient to attest that Jesus was the Messiah. After the blind man had returned from the pool of Siloam, and had been interrogated by the Pharisees, the Messiah met with him again, and asked, *"Do you believe on the Son of God?"* The newly healed man asked his interrogator to

13   Sanhedrin 7.4 A & D (Mishnah).
14   cf. Luke 4:41.

identify the Son of God. Jesus replied, *"You have both seen Him, and it is He who is talking with you."* With the words, *"I believe"*, he worshipped (9:35-38).

The raising of Lazarus contains two references to Jesus as the Son of God. The first is the prophecy that the sickness and death of Lazarus will be used to the glory of the Son of God (John 11:4). The second comes in the confession of Martha, *"I believe that You are the Christ, the Son of God"* (John 11:27).

Only in the episode with the man born blind does the Messiah claim to be the Son of God, but in none of the episodes does He deny it. In all of these incidents He accepts the title.

Jesus the Great I AM.

Then there is the use of "εγω ειμι", "I AM". John's liberal use of this phrase in the narrative of the Messiah's life is designed to indicate that Jesus was the incarnation of the God of Israel. The strongest example is in chapter 8: *"Jesus said to them, Most assuredly* [Truly, truly], *I say to you, before Abraham was* [born], *I AM"* (John 8:58). The double "amen" (translated "truly, truly"), at the beginning of the declaration emphasizes its importance. The use of the phrase "I AM" points back to the theophany at the burning bush, where YHWH gave Moses a revelation of His eternal, yet ever in the present, nature: "I AM WHO I AM" (Ex. 3:14). This is further concentrated and used as a personal name of God. YHWH instructed Moses to use the name "I AM" to identify to Israel the God of Abraham, Isaac and Jacob: *"And God said to Moses, 'I AM WHO I AM'. And He said, 'Thus you shall say to the children of Israel, I AM has sent me to you. Moreover God said to Moses, Thus you shall say to the children of Israel: The Lord God of your fathers, the God of Abraham, the God of Isaac, and the God of Jacob, has sent me to you. This is My name forever, and this is My memorial to all generations'"* (Ex. 3:14-15). Jesus' appropriation of this great name of God to Himself was a claim to deity: *"Then* [the Jews] *picked up stones to throw at Him"* (John 8:59).

The apostle John opens his gospel with a series of statements that declare that Jesus is the source, giver and sustainer of all life, natural and spiritual, temporal and eternal (John 1:1-14). With this truth always uppermost in his mind, John included the "I AM" sayings of Jesus, together with the discourses that were their context, to demonstrate how dependent we are on Jesus as the fountainhead of our spiritual life.

"*I AM the bread of life*" (John 6:35,48,51) is set in the context of the **incarnation**:[15] "*I AM the living bread which came down from heaven.*"

"*I AM the light of the world*" (John 8:12; 9:5; 12:46) is set in the context of the then current **ministry** of the Messiah: "*As long as I am in the world, I AM the light of the world.*"

"*I AM the door of the sheep*" (John 10:7,9) and "*I AM the good shepherd*" (John 10:11,14) are set in the context of the **death** of Christ (v. 15): "*I AM the good shepherd. The good shepherd gives His life for the sheep.*"

"*I AM the resurrection and the life*" (John 11:25) is set in the context of **resurrection** (vv. 23-24): "*Jesus said to her, Your brother will rise again.*"

"*I AM the way, the truth, and the life*" (John 14:6) is set in the context of the **ascension** of Christ: "*Let not your heart be troubled; you believe in God, believe also in Me. In My Father's house are many mansions; if it were not so, I would have told you. I go to prepare a place for you*" (vv. 1-2).

"*I AM the vine*" (John 15:1,5) is set in the context of a promised **pentecost**: "*But when the Helper [Comforter] comes, whom I shall send to you from the Father, the Spirit of truth, who proceeds from the Father, he will testify of Me*" (v. 26); "*Nevertheless I tell you the truth. It is to your advantage that I go away: for if I go not away, the Helper will not come to you; but if I depart, I will send Him to you*" (John 16:7).

This set of self-revelatory statements by the incarnate God encompasses elements from the whole cycle of the earthly life of the Messiah (from heaven to earth to heaven)—the incarnation, ministry, death, resurrection, ascension, return to the Father and the outpouring of the Holy Spirit. Individually the "I AM" statements are impressive, but as a group of interlocking truths they are compelling.

For each of these statements to begin with the name of God that indicates His eternal nature must mean that they are completely

---

15   John 6:33,35,38,41-42,51.

in harmony with the character and essence of the eternal God. They were not offices that the Son of God simply embraced in His incarnate state. For example, He was the Good Shepherd before ever He was born in a stable and visited by under-shepherds. In the "Good Shepherd" discourse, He stated that He would give His life for the sheep. Peter said it was in fulfilment of a plan devised before the creation of the world. He wrote, *"...knowing that you were not redeemed with corruptible things, like silver or gold...but with the precious blood of Christ, as of a lamb without blemish and without spot. He indeed was foreordained before the foundation of the world, but was manifest in these last times for you"* (1 Pet. 1:18-20). Furthermore, the gospel writer John indicated that His sacrifice is eternally a part of His person and work. In the throne-room of heaven, he saw the *"Lion of the tribe of Juda, the Root of David"* as a newly slain lamb, at the heart of the government of God (Rev. 4:5-6).

And when Jesus said *"I AM the light of the world"*, He implied that He was, is and always would be the light of the world. John expressed it in His prologue when He said Jesus was the true Light who *"gives light to every man coming into the world"* (John 1:9).

Jesus Christ is the *"I AM"*. He is God, eternally the same, yesterday, today and forever.

The next strongest, and most obvious connection (after John 8:58) between the Messiah of the New Testament and the *"I AM"* of the Old Testament is given in the statement, *"I AM the resurrection and the life."* The Sadducees, in their conflict with Jesus, challenged Him regarding the truth of the resurrection. He responded by stating that in the Pentateuch, the resurrection is seen most clearly in the statement, *"I AM the God of Abraham, the God of Isaac, and the God of Jacob."*[16] Jesus adding the words, *"He is not the God of the dead, but of the living"*.

This interpretation of Exodus 3:6 came afresh to those who heard Him that day. Whether it was already the teaching of the Rabbis is uncertain. We know that it was their position at a much later date because of the commentary of R. Abin on Exodus 32:13, in which he narrates that Moses enquired of God,

---

16   Matt. 22:32; Mark 12:26; Luke 20:37.

"O Eternal God, do those live who are dead?"
"Yes", saith God.
Then saith Moses, "If those that are dead do live, remember Abraham, Isaac, and Jacob."[17]

The "ɪ ᴀᴍ" who called Moses is the God of the resurrection. The executive arm of the Godhead who will raise the dead is Jesus the Messiah. In the passage in which He stated, *"ɪ ᴀᴍ the bread of life"*, He dealt with the matter of eternal life and declared, *"And this is the will of Him who sent Me, that everyone who sees the Son and believes in Him may have everlasting life, and I will raise him up at the last day"* (John 6:40, ɴᴀsʙ). This truth was further emphasized (vv. 39,44,54). He said at another time: *"For the hour is coming, in which all who are in the graves will hear His* [the Son of Man's] *voice, and come forth—those who have done good, to the resurrection of life, and those who have done evil, to the resurrection of condemnation"* (John 5:28-29). His power to raise all the dead is a demonstration of His omnipotence. His power to separate those who did good deeds from those who did evil deeds is a demonstration of His omniscience.

There are several further texts in John's gospel which include the absolute use of "ἐγω εἰμι" (ɪ ᴀᴍ). They are: 4:26; 6:20; 8:24,58; 13:19; 18:5-6,8. Each of these is illuminating.

In response to the woman at the well in John 4 when she said, *"I know that Messiah is coming (who is called Christ). When He comes, He will tell us all things."* Jesus said to her, *"Ἐγώ εἰμι, ὁ λαλῶν σοι"* (John 4:26). Young's literal translation renders it as *"ɪ ᴀᴍ [he] who am speaking unto thee."*

To the distressed disciples when they saw Jesus walking over the sea to them in the night, He said, *"Ἐγώ εἰμι· μὴ φοβεῖσθε."* *"ɪ ᴀᴍ [he]. Be not afraid"* (John 6:20, Young's).

In a warning to the Jews He said, *"Ye shall die in your sins: for if ye believe not that ɪ ᴀᴍ* [ἐγώ εἰμι] *[he], ye shall die in your sins"* (John 8:24, Young's).

The reference, John 8:58, is the cornerstone text, *"πρὶν Ἀβραὰμ γενέσθαι ἐγὼ εἰμί."* *"Before Abraham was ɪ ᴀᴍ."*

17 The Treasury of Scripture Knowledge: Five Hundred Thousand Scripture Reference and Parallel Passages. (Oak Harbor: Logos Research Systems, Inc., 1995), Luke 20:37.

At the last supper He offered to His disciples advance notice of the fulfilment of prophecy as evidence of His deity. *"Now I tell you before it comes, that when it does come to pass, you may believe that I AM He"* (ἐγώ εἰμι) (John 13:19).

In the garden when they came to arrest Him with more than 500 combat troops at their disposal, John records the use of the absolute *"ἐγώ εἰμι"* (I AM) as His identifying response (18:5-6,8). His use of the Name caused Judas and the front ranks of Jews to draw back and fall to the ground.

Jesus was identified as the great *"I AM"* to Samaritans and Jews, friends and enemies, a title which was a comfort to His friends but a terror to His enemies.

When the nation's leaders investigated His Messianic credentials, Jesus claimed a particular prerogative of deity, namely, the ability to forgive sins. He said to an obdurate sinner, *"your sins are forgiven you"* (Matt. 9:2). The Sanhedrists correctly asserted that none could forgive sins but God only. Jesus forgave the sins of the paralytic; therefore, Jesus claimed deity.

Furthermore, in the upper room discourse He said He would send the Holy Spirit which would be impossible if He were not God (John 15:26).

Chapter 3

What Evidence was the Messiah Expected to Provide to Support His Claim?

The High Priest, the Chief Priests and many other members of the Sanhedrin were completely unprepared, unable, and most significantly, unqualified, to evaluate the incarnate Son of God's claim to deity. These were not spiritual men. The principle, *"A natural man does not accept the things of the Spirit of God, for they are foolishness to him; and he cannot understand them, because they are spiritually appraised"* (1 Cor. 2:14 NASB), was evident. On the other hand, as students of the T'nach they knew what to look for in any Messianic claimant. They expected attesting miracles. *"The Jews require a sign,"* wrote Paul (1 Cor. 1:22 KJV). The Messiah provided multiple miracles to answer this requirement.

Initially, the identifying signs of the Messiah were the same as those primary signs of Israel's first Messiah/Deliverer, Moses. He had said, *"The Lord your God will raise up for you a Prophet like me from your midst, from your brethren. Him you shall hear"* (Deut. 18:15). God's choice of attesting signs of Messiahship for Moses was not a random selection. The circumstances of Adam's transgression in the Garden of Eden dictated that God's Messiah would have to demonstrate that He had the power to deliver from the effects of the fall. Namely, He would obtain victory over Satan where Adam knew defeat; and He would provide forgiveness of sin where Satan had promoted judgment. This could not be accomplished without cost, as the key Genesis 3:15 prophecy indicates. The seed of the woman would crush the serpent's head, but the serpent would crush the heel of the woman's seed. In other words, the Devil would inflict a severe wound on the Messiah and the Messiah would inflict a mortal wound on Satan. The design of the Messianic miracles therefore, had to symbolize (1) the subjugation of Satan, (2a) authority to judge sin, (2b) authority to forgive sin, and (3) the ultimate defeat of Satan at personal cost to the Messiah.

God gave Moses power to perform such authenticating miracles as were needed to convince the elders of Israel that YHWH had commissioned him to deliver them from slavery. These miracles were later reinforced by other additional signs when God dealt with Pharaoh's hard-hearted opposition, and when He miraculously sustained the nation as they journeyed through the inhospitable territory of the Sinai desert.

The Sanhedrin expected Messianic claimants to perform miracles of the calibre of the primary attesting signs of Moses, as well as other miraculous works.

While the ministry of Moses was accredited by miracles that had the symbolism of future truth (they were a type or shadow of future reality), the signs authenticating the ministry of the Redeemer of Israel had to be of the same character, but much more. The Messiah's miracles were the anti-type, the reality of that which had been foreshadowed. It was not enough that His miracles should imply He was more powerful than the Devil, they should demonstrate the impotence of Satan in His presence and be part of the victory. His signs should not simply symbolize the forgiveness of sin; they should display His authority to forgive sin.

What is involved here is a matter of life and death. In the Garden, Satan, the Father of lies, said, *"You will not surely die"* (Gen. 3:4). Moses, the historian, in the first volume of the Pentateuch, highlights the veracity of God and the mendacity of the Devil. The life-spans of the Patriarchs are listed with the refrain, *"and he died"*. The early history includes a global demonstration of the catastrophic effect of sin: *"...all in whose nostrils was the breath of life died..."* (Gen. 7:22). Against this dark backdrop, the miraculous ministry of the Messiah must be life-imparting, life-affirming and life-improving. The result of His ministry must be, *"in Christ* [Messiah] *all shall be made alive"* (1 Cor. 15:22).

The First Primary Attesting Sign: The Serpent in Subjection.

Because of his activity in Eden, the serpent was "cursed" and punished. Since it had exalted itself above its allotted estate, God threw it to the ground, commanding, *"on your belly you shall go"* (Gen. 3:14), imposing the mark of deepest degradation (Lev. 11:42). However, when God spoke to the reptile, and pronounced a curse upon it, He was not addressing the irrational beast so much as the spiritual Tempter. The punishment that fell upon the serpent was merely a symbol of the punishment of the unseen agent of evil. The prophecy of Genesis 3:15, supported by later clarifying Scriptures, makes it clear that the casting down of the serpent was in fact a judgment on Satan: *"I will put enmity between you and the woman, and between your seed and her Seed; he shall bruise your head, and you shall bruise His heel."* Keil and Delitzsch in their commentary suggest the construction of the Hebrew clarifies who is in view in the prophecy[18]. In examining Genesis 3:15, they observe that in the first clause, the seed of the serpent is opposed to the seed of the woman, but in the second clause, the seed of the woman gains victory over the serpent itself. *"It* [the seed of the woman] *will crush your head, and you* [not your seed] *will crush its heel."* Thus the seed of the serpent is hidden behind the unity of the serpent, or rather of the foe who, through the serpent, has done such injury to man. This foe is Satan, who incessantly opposes the seed of the woman and bruises its heel, but is eventually to be trodden under its feet. The death of the Messiah is in view here.

To equate the Edenic serpent with Satan is scriptural. The book of Revelation describes the Prince of fallen angels as, *"the great dragon"* and, *"that serpent of old"*, and gives his names, *"the Devil, and Satan"* (Rev. 12:9; 20:2). The casting down of the serpent in the Garden, representing the casting down of Satan,

---

18   C.F. Keil & F. Delitzsch, Commentary on the Old Testament, Electronic Edition. (Peabody: Hendrickson Publishers Inc., 2002) Gen. 3:15.

followed an earlier event that the Messiah had witnessed: *"I beheld Satan as lightning fall from heaven"* (Luke 10:18 KJV). Ezekiel described it more fully:

> *Therefore I cast you as a profane thing*
> *Out of the mountain of God;*
> *And I destroyed you, O covering cherub,*
> *From the midst of the fiery stones.*
> *Your heart was lifted up because of your beauty;*
> *You corrupted your wisdom for the sake of your splendor;*
> *I cast you to the ground,* (Ez. 28:16-17).

Here, God judged pride and undisciplined personal ambition. The language of this prophecy, while naming the king of Tyre, rises beyond any earthly ruler to describe events surrounding the fall of Satan. There are further defeats for Satan yet to come and he will be thrown down again to the earth (Rev. 12:9), and again into the bottomless pit (Rev. 20:3), and again into the lake of fire (v. 10).

The first attesting sign given to Moses was for a symbolic re-enactment of the casting down of Satan, to demonstrate the power and authority of God over the Devil, a power and authority delegated to His chosen servant.

> *So the Lord said to him, "What is that in your hand?" He said, "A rod." And He said, "Cast it on the ground." So he cast it on the ground, and it became a serpent; and Moses fled from it. Then the Lord said to Moses, "Reach out your hand and take it by the tail" (and he reached out his hand and caught it, and it became a rod in his hand), "that they may believe that the Lord God of their fathers, the God of Abraham, the God of Isaac, and the God of Jacob, has appeared to you" (Ex. 4:2-5).*

Not only did Moses enact this for the elders of Israel, but he also re-enacted it before Pharaoh. The Pharaohs of Egypt wore the image of a serpent on their diadem, as the symbol of royal and divine power. The Pharaoh, before whom Moses and Aaron appeared, was Satan's instrument to hold God's people in slavery. The grip of Satan had to be broken if the nation of Israel were to be freed. The first act of Israel's Deliverer was a challenge to Satan. Aaron cast down Moses' rod, symbol of the defeat of Satan, and it became a serpent. The court sorcerers imitated the miracle with their rods, which also became serpents. However, Moses with the delegated power of God at his disposal, had control, not only over his serpent but also over the serpents of the court magicians. This meant he had power over the Egyptian sorcerers too. Pharaoh's attempt to discredit the sign failed. Moses' power over the serpents and the court magicians further implied power over Pharaoh, Satan's tool, and beyond that, power over Satan.

The Second Primary Attesting Sign: Mastery Over Leprosy

Because of Satanic activity, our first parents disobeyed the clear command of God and incurred the consequence that God said would follow, *"...in the day that you eat of it you shall surely die"* (Gen. 2:17). They did not immediately fall to ground but were subject to a "living death", a process of dying; the Hebrew could be translated, "dying you will die". Leprosy, also called "the living death", was considered a visual of the stroke of God in the Garden. The Hebrew for leprosy, *"tsara'ath"*, is related to the Arabic word that signifies "to strike down or scourge". *Tsara'ath* (leprosy) is considered the scourge of God. This truth is re-emphasized in the T'nach where God judged individuals who rebelled against His will and struck them with leprosy. When Miriam rebelled, *"...the anger of the LORD was aroused...and...suddenly, Miriam became leprous, as white as snow"* (Num. 12:9-10). Uzziah contracted leprosy when he discarded the priestly protocol contained in the Mosaic law: *"leprosy broke out on his forehead...because the LORD had struck him"* (2 Chron. 26:19-20 KJV).

Two words that are strongly connected with leprosy are *"naga"* (touch, reach, strike); and its derivative *"nega"* (stroke, plague, disease). In Leviticus chapter 13, there are instructions for the diagnosis of leprosy, and in chapter 14 instructions for the performing of the rituals required in the case of recovered lepers. In these two chapters *"nega"*, translated "plague" in the KJV and sometimes "plague" and sometimes "sore" in the NKJV, is used some eighty times. Again, the connection is—the plague (*nega*) of leprosy is the visual of the stroke of God. In Isaiah 53, both these words occur, but there the plague is sin, and because of that plague, God's Messiah must suffer God's stroke. Of the Suffering Servant it says, *"He was cut off out of the land of the living for the transgression of my people, to whom the stroke was due"* (Isa. 53:8 NASB). And again, *"Surely he has borne our griefs, and carried our sorrows: yet we esteemed Him stricken, smitten by God, and afflicted"* (v. 4). One commentary suggests that "in every other passage in which it does not occur in the special sense of leprosy, [it] points back to the generic idea of a plague divinely sent."[19] So strong was the connection of leprosy to sin, and because these words, which were frequently used in the special case of leprosy, were used of the Suffering Servant, some ancients implied that the Messiah became leprous. This, of course, has no scriptural warrant. Nevertheless, it identifies the strong connection of sin to leprosy and is further evidence that leprosy was accepted as the visual manifestation of the stroke of God against sin.

According to the Pentateuch, it was the duty of the priests to *"distinguish between holy and unholy and between unclean and clean"* (Lev. 10:10-11). Since leprosy was emblematic of sin (that is, the outward and visible sign of inner spiritual corruption), the leper was "unclean" as well as ill; "unclean" here being associated with "unholy". If he recovered, the priest would declare him "clean". Being unclean/unholy, separated the leper from the Tabernacle, from the Temple, from God, and from God's people. The Rabbis traced disease to moral causes: "no death without sin, and no pain without transgression",[20] so they took a mainly moral view of the disease and only secondarily a sanitary view. Because leprosy represented sin, the priest could not pronounce a recovered leper clean until atonement had been made for his soul. The ceremony included, on the first day, two clean birds, one sacrificed and one set free; and on the eighth day a trespass offering, a sin offering, a meat offering and a burnt offering.

The instructions in the Law demanded that the leper be separated from ordinary social contact, with the further require-

19   C.F. Keil & F. Delitzsch, Isa. 53:8.
20   Shabbat 5a (Babylonian Tamud).

ment that he had to warn any who came near that to touch him would render them unclean, defiled, and unholy.

Here then is the sense of the second attesting sign for God's Deliverer—he must have mastery over leprosy, symbolizing that he has the answer to sin. He must be able to cleanse the defiled and return the sinner to fellowship both with God and with the people of God. Accordingly, God said to Moses, *"'Now put your hand in your bosom.' And he put his hand in his bosom, and when he took it out, behold, his hand was leprous, like snow. And He said, 'Put your hand in your bosom again.' So he put his hand in his bosom again, and drew it out of his bosom, and behold, it was restored like his other flesh. 'Then it will be, if they do not believe you, nor heed the message of the first sign, that they may believe the message of the latter sign'"* (Ex. 4:6-8).

It should not be overlooked that the sign involving leprosy was both positive and negative. The personal action of Moses both inflicted leprosy and healed it. This suggests not only the possibility of forgiveness for sin but also punishment for sin. The examples of Miriam, Uzziah and Gehazi are pertinent here. God, through Moses, incorporated the principle suggested by this sign into the legal framework imposed on the Jewish nation. The Law was the agent to awaken the knowledge of sin (Rom. 3:20). Before the Law, sin was not imputed to the sinner, but it was the introduction of the Law that made him culpable (Rom. 5:13). So, if on the one hand animal sacrifices could obtain forgiveness for sin, on the other hand, failure to comply with the Law carried with it severe penalties, even capital punishment. For example, *"You shall keep the Sabbath, for it is holy to you. Everyone who profanes it shall surely be put to death; for whoever does any work on it, that person shall be cut off from among his people"* (Ex. 31:14).[21]

The Third Primary Attesting Sign: Water into Blood

The two signs should have been sufficient, but in the event that the elders asked for another, God provided one more. He said, *"Then it will be, if they do not believe you, nor heed the message of the first sign, that they may believe the message of the latter sign.*

---

21   cf. Ex. 12:15,19; 30:33,38; Lev. 7:20-21,25,27; 17:4,9,14.

And it shall be, if they do not believe even these two signs, or listen to your voice, that you shall take water from the river and pour it on the dry land. The water which you take from the river will become blood on the dry land" (Ex. 4:8-9).

Since *"the life of the flesh is in the blood"*(Lev. 17:11 NASB),[22] spilt blood means a life taken. The first Biblical reference to blood on the ground is the record of a violent, premature death. The spilt blood of Abel had a voice that called for justice against his murderer: *"And* [the Lord] *said, 'What have you done? The voice of your brother's blood cries out to Me from the ground'"* (Gen. 4:10). In the last book of the Bible the example is repeated, where the blood of the martyrs calls for justice (Rev 6:9-10). When Moses poured out water from the Nile, it too became blood on the ground and because of the slaughter of the innocents, when young male Israelite babies were murdered in its waters, its voice also cried to God for justice against Pharaoh (Ex. 1:22). If the elders of Israel will not call for a Deliverer to deal with the Egyptian ruler, then the blood of the innocents will! This truth would not escape Moses since he had himself been abandoned to the Nile.

Furthermore, if the blood were the blood of a sacrifice, then that would be evidence that an animal had died a substitutionary death. This, in fact, is the context of the Leviticus quotation, *"for the life of the flesh is in the blood"*, for the text continues, *"and I have given it to you upon the altar to make atonement for your souls; for it is the blood that makes atonement for the soul"* (Lev. 17:11).

The book of Genesis is the narrative of how death reigned because sin reigned (Rom. 5:13-14). But in amongst the record of the decease of countless individuals, there are other events that indicate how both physical and spiritual death would, in due course, be conquered. They point to overcoming death by:

1. substitution—the ram in place of Isaac (Gen. 22:13);
2. translation—Enoch leaving earth for heaven without dying (Gen. 5:24);
3. preservation—Noah and his family preserved in the ark when everyone else died (Gen. 7:1 ff);
4. resurrection—Abraham believed that God would raise

---

22   cf. Gen. 9:4,5; Lev. 17:14; Deut. 12:23.

his son, Isaac, from the dead (Heb. 11:19).

Since the third sign is blood on the ground, we turn our attention to the truth of substitution, for it alone involves the shedding of blood. This is in harmony with the narrative in Genesis, for the truth of "substitution" has precedence, first by implication when animal skins were supplied to "cover" the shame of Adam and Eve (Gen. 3:21); and then more clearly in the sacrifice of lambs by Abel (Gen. 4:4), and then most clearly in the substitution of a ram for Isaac (Gen. 22:13).

Then in Exodus, the substitutionary death of a sacrifice became the cornerstone of the Mosaic economy. Examples include the substitutionary death of what later came to be known as the "Passover lamb". Each family was required to kill a perfect lamb, and then to ritually paint its blood on the lintel and two side posts of the doorway to their home. This would protect the first-born of the family from the stroke of God. The "covering" of the first-born by spilt blood was such a momentous event that it was to be remembered and celebrated annually until the substitutionary Lamb of God, Jesus Messiah, died for the sins of the world (1 Cor. 5:7). Moreover, His sacrificial, substitutionary death which replaced the sacrifice of the Passover lamb, is itself commemorated in the ordinance of the Church in the sharing of bread and wine in a symbolic feast.

Out of the exodus of Israel from Egypt arose a whole raft of new laws that related to the moral and spiritual state of the nation. These included many more substitutionary offerings. These offerings indicated that Moses had some means of dealing with sin that allowed Israelite offenders to be cleansed from defilement and restored to fellowship with God. Under the Levitical code, the last two of the five sacrificial offerings, the trespass offering (Lev. 5) and the sin offering (Lev. 4), were to make propitiation and expiation for sin. While they are the last named in the short catalogue of five offerings to the Lord, they were usually offered first. The sacrifice of the trespass offering appeased YHWH for sins committed. The sacrifice of the sin offering obtained forgiveness for the sinner. The first dealt with the sinful actions of the Israelite, the second dealt with his sinful condition. These offerings were, of course, only a temporary answer to sin. Animal blood could never remove sin—only cover it (Heb. 10:4,11). It is the blood of Jesus/Messiah, God's Son, which alone atones for sin and restores the sinner (Heb. 10:10-14).

And let us not fail to notice that the third attesting sign used water. Under Torah regulations, the primary cleansing agent is blood. Ritual purity needed blood rather than water, for *"according to the law almost all things are purified with blood, and without shedding of blood there is no remission"* (Heb. 9:22). But sometimes water was the cleansing agent. The rules of ablution, incorporating the constant bathing of the priests and the washing of vessels, were particularly strict. The national place of worship, the Tabernacle, had two pieces of furniture in the outer court, a laver and an altar. In the ritual that took place in the Tabernacle, the laver provided the cleansing agent—water, and the sacrificial altar provided the cleansing agent—blood.

There were times when the ritual needed both blood and water. For example, the leper needed both to be clean: *"He who is to be cleansed shall wash his clothes, shave off all his hair, and wash himself in water, that he may be clean. After that he shall come into the camp, and shall stay outside his tent seven days"* (Lev. 14:8). Then *"the priest shall take some of the blood of the trespass offering, and the priest shall put it on the tip of the right ear of him who is to be cleansed, on the thumb of his right hand, and on the big toe of his right foot"* (v. 14). Also, the ritual for the cleansing of a house used the two agents, blood and water. *"And he shall cleanse the house with the blood of the bird and the running water and the living bird, with the cedar wood, the hyssop, and the scarlet"* (v. 52).

The Signs as Forensic Evidence

The language used of the attesting signs is the language used of witnesses. The KJV uses the word "voice"—*"the voice of the first sign"* and *"the voice of the latter sign"*. Under the Mosaic Law, two witnesses were enough for a matter to be established (Deut. 19:15). The first of the two witnesses was Moses (*"if they will not believe...your voice"*). The witness of Moses was his testimony. He had been present at the miracle of the burning bush, he had heard the voice of God, he had received the attesting signs, and YHWH had commissioned him (Ex. 3:1 ff). The second voice was the witness of the first of the miraculous acts that God had given Moses to perform before the elders of Israel, that is, the casting down of the rod to change it into a serpent.

Three witnesses would be stronger (Deut. 19:15), namely, (i) the testimony of Moses, (ii) the sign of the serpent rod—the first attesting sign, and (iii) the sign of leprosy inflicted and cured—the second attesting sign. If they refused the testimony of the three witnesses, then God instructed Moses to take water from the Nile and turn it into blood on the ground. This sign later became the first plague. Moreover, when he changed the water of the river (itself widely used as a cleansing agent) into blood, (the primary ritual cleansing agent), he foreshadowed an act of the Lord Jesus. John chapter 2 describes how the Messiah changed the water, used for the Jewish rites of purification, into wine that would be used by the Messiah to symbolize His spilt blood, which was shed as the cleansing agent for sin.

So Moses had four "voices" to testify that he was God's chosen Deliverer. Two or three witnesses would have been enough but YHWH provided four—four is the number of completeness—there was no doubt!

Summary of the four voices (witnesses).
1. The personal eyewitness testimony of Moses.
2. The first attesting sign—the serpent rod miracle—symbolizing the serpent in subjection (i.e. victory over Satan)
3. The second attesting sign—leprosy inflicted and cured—symbolizing sin imputed and cleansed.
4. The third attesting sign—water becoming blood on the ground—representing violent, premature, death, which will be the cost paid for victory over Satan (first attesting sign) and the cleansing from sin (second attesting sign).

The Acceptance of the Authenticating Signs
Moses performed the signs for the elders and convinced them of God's intentions (Ex. 4:29-31). The attesting signs had accomplished their purpose, and Israel's leaders accepted Moses

as God's choice to be Guide, Deliverer and Mediator for Israel. Other miracles followed in the wake of the primary, authenticating signs, such as the plagues upon the Egyptians (from blood throughout Egypt to the death of the firstborn), and blessings on Israel (the living water from the rock, and bread from heaven). But these were subsequent to, and consequent of, the major attesting signs.

Having isolated the principle attesting signs of Messiahship, we can now return to our inquiry. What evidence did Jesus offer to support His claim that He was, in fact, the Messiah, prophesied by Moses and timetabled by Gabriel through Daniel?

1. Did He have a personal eyewitness testimony similar to Moses?
2. Did He have the serpent in subjection? That is, did He have power over Satan?
3. Did He have mastery over leprosy? That is, did He have the answer to sin?
4. Would there be blood on the ground? That is, would He pay the price?

With respect to question 1, on many occasions Jesus testified of His personal relationship with God, using the phrase "my Father" frequently,[23]—but the focus of our inquiry is the physical evidence of the signs (Nos. 2, 3 & 4).

---

23   35 times in John's Gospel, including "*I and my Father are one*" (John 10:30).

Chapter 4
Authenticating Miracles in the Synoptic Gospels

Prologue to the First Attesting Sign: The Serpent in Subjection

As Pharaoh had Israel in bondage in Egypt, so the Devil held Israel captive in the land of promise. To liberate Israel, Moses had to overcome Pharaoh, the servant of Satan, but in the greater conflict between light and darkness, good and evil, Jesus had to overthrow Satan himself. Therefore, before the public ministry of the Messiah could take place, Jesus had to face the evil one in the wilderness. The Bible says He was "led" there to face the Lord of Evil. Matthew and Luke give us the most details of the conflict.

In both accounts, the first temptation is the challenge to turn stone into bread. Jesus countered with a quote from the T'nach: *"It is written, Man shall not live by bread alone, but by every word of God"* (Luke 4:4; Matt. 4:4). The passage from which this quote was taken is in Deuteronomy chapter 8. *"And you shall remember that **the Lord** your God **led you** all the way these forty years in the wilderness, to humble you and **test you**, to know what was in your heart, whether you would keep His commandments or not. So He humbled you, **allowed you to hunger**, and fed you with manna which you did not know nor did your fathers know, that **He might make you know that man shall not live by bread alone; but man lives by every word that proceeds from the mouth of the Lord"* (Deut. 8:2-3). Observe the highlighted words: *"the Lord... led you...to test you...He allowed you to hunger...that He might* *make you know that man shall not live by bread alone; but man lives by every word that proceeds from the mouth of the Lord."* The Messiah, recalling the events of the 40-year wilderness experience of Israel, and comparing them to His 40-day wilderness experience, concluded that in a similar manner the Spirit of God had led him there to test Him. It was God Himself who permitted, nay required Him, to be hungry. To yield to the insinuation that He would benefit by stepping outside the revealed will of God would alienate Him from His Father. As the last Adam He would have failed in a similar manner to the first Adam. What Satan did not include in his calculations was the fact that performing the will of God is both physically and spiritually nourishing. Jesus Himself speaks of it at another time when He was again hungry and thirsty, *"My food is to do the will of Him who sent Me, and to finish His work"* (John 4:34). Since His condition was in the will of God, to seek to alleviate His hunger would put personal comfort above the purposes of God, and would equate to disobedience of the command of God. Jesus understood that His experience was not simply the enmity of the Adversary, but also a test from God as to whether He would keep His Father's commandments, do His Father's will. The quote from the Torah was enough to close that avenue of temptation.

In the Garden of Eden, the pre-incarnate Christ cast down the serpent, symbolically demonstrating His power over Satan, the "cast down" one.[24] In preparation for the exodus from Egypt, Moses, commissioned by God as Deliverer, re-enacted this same scene and the serpent was again "cast down", re-affirming the continuing power and authority of God over Satan. The ministry of the *"seed of the woman"* must demonstrate this same power and authority, and climax in the prophesied *"bruising"* of the serpent's head (Gen. 3:15). However, the enemy of the Messiah is the Devil, who operates on the principle of "deception with a view to destruction". It was his *modus operandi* in the Garden.

Jesus referred to this element of deception when He said to the Jews of His generation, *"You are of your father the devil, and the desires of your father you want to do....When he speaks a lie,*

---

24   Satan had already been cast down out of heaven. Cf. Luke 10:18.

he speaks from his own resources, for he is a liar and the father of it" (John 8:44). We are warned of the *"wiles of the devil"* (Eph. 6:11). His followers are *"deceitful workers, transforming themselves into apostles of Christ. And no wonder! For Satan himself transforms himself into an angel of light"* (2 Cor. 11:13-14).

However, it is deception with a view to destruction. Not only is he the father of lies but also a *"murderer from the beginning"* (John 8:44). He is the Adversary, *"a roaring lion"* who goes about *"seeking whom he may devour"* (1 Pet. 5:8).

It is this deceiver, in the "one-to-one", "face-to-face" confrontation with the incarnate God, who attempts to cloud the issue and misdirect the Messiah into taking the position of the one "cast down". Satan took Jesus up a very high mountain, showed Him all the splendour of the kingdoms of the world, and said, *"All these things I will give You if You will fall down and worship me"* (Matt. 4:8-9; Luke 4:5-6). It was inevitable that Satan would couch this temptation in terms that reflected the cause of his own downfall—personal ambition running counter to the will of God. Here he tries to recover all lost ground with one throw of the dice. What he had failed to do when he was the mighty, covering cherub, he tried to accomplish when the God that defeated him there was clothed in flesh. Jesus, weak with hunger, refused the offer and put His finger on the crux of the matter: *"Away with you, Satan! For it is written, 'You shall worship the Lord your God, and Him only you shall serve'"* (Matt. 4:10). Jesus rejected the offer of kingdoms, power and glory; and later reminded His followers that, *"the kingdom, and the power and the glory"* eternally belong to the Father (Matt. 6:13).

In the third of the temptations, Satan took Jesus to the top of the tower on the southwestern corner of the Temple Mount, where he challenged Him, *"If You are the Son of God, throw* [cast] *Yourself down. For it is written: 'He shall give His angels charge over you', and, 'In their hands they shall bear you up, Lest you dash your foot against a stone'"* (Matt. 4:6; Luke 4:9-11). This less than subtle effort was another attempt to get Jesus, Son of God, to occupy the position of the one "cast down". Israel's Messiah, who must have been meditating on the trials and difficulties of Moses, His Messianic predecessor, responded to the Devil with another quote from Deuteronomy: *"You shall not tempt the Lord your God."*[25] The full quote is, *"You shall not tempt the Lord your God as you tempted Him in Massah."* Massah is the Hebrew word for "tempted", as recorded in Exodus: *"So he called the name of the place Massah…because of the contention of the children of Israel, and because they tempted the Lord, saying, 'Is the Lord among us or not?'"* (Ex. 17:7). Jesus, recalling this episode from the history of the wandering nation, used the quote from the speech of Moses to repulse the temptation, and affirm that God was with Him — a powerful response to the conditional challenge, *"If You are the Son of God"*. James encapsulated the essence of the narrative recorded here when he wrote, *"…submit to God. Resist the devil and he will flee from you"* (Jas. 4:7).

After Satan had left Him, and angels had ministered to Him, He *"returned in the power of the Spirit to Galilee, and news of Him went out through all the surrounding region"* (Luke 4:14).

The First Attesting Sign: The Serpent in Subjection

Luke, who testified that he put his gospel in chronological order (1:1), used an event in which Jesus laid out His claim to be Messiah, to introduce the healing of a man with the spirit of an unclean devil. After the conflict with Satan in the wilderness, during which the Devil unsuccessfully tried to make Jesus the "cast down" One, the carpenter's Son presented Himself to His home congregation as Messiah (Luke 4:16-21).[26] When the congregation questioned His authority to make such a claim Jesus sensed their unbelief and responded, *"No prophet is accepted in his own country"* (v. 24). He followed this statement with two examples of prophets ministering to Gentiles while Israel was in unbelief. Those people who had been fellow citizens of His in Nazareth were filled with a demonic fury and *"rose up and thrust Him out of the city; and they led Him to the brow of the hill on which their city was built, that they might throw Him down over the cliff"* (v. 29). Having failed to manipulate the Messiah into being the "cast down" one, here Satan inspired those who had been His neighbours, His customers, His friends, to enact it. It was

---

25   Matt. 4:7; Luke 4:12; Deut. 6:16.
26   see also Luke 2.

another attempt to kill Him before His time and by a method that would reverse the prophecy of God. To bruise Satan's head, Jesus would have to be the "lifted up" One. The people of Nazareth tried to make Him the "cast down" One. Jesus *passing through the midst of them he went His way"* (Luke 4:30). A similar incident took place later in His ministry where He coined the more famous phrase that has now become a proverb: *"A prophet is not without honour except in his own country"* (Mark 6:4; Matt. 13:57). To that incident, the writer added the post-script: *"He did not do many mighty works there because of their unbelief."*

Rejected in Nazareth, the Messiah travelled to Capernaum, where in the synagogue, a man with the spirit of an unclean devil was troubled at the presence of the One who is stronger that Satan (Luke 4:33-36; 11:20-22). Jesus commanded the demon, *"Be quiet and come out of him"* (Luke 4:35). With a last defiant flourish, it "cast down" the poor, possessed individual and then left him. This demonstration of Messianic control over Satan amazed everyone in the synagogue who talked of His authority and power.

Lightfoot points out that the phrasing of Scripture at this place is quite significant.[27] The man had "a spirit of an unclean devil." The Jews made a difference between an unclean spirit and an evil spirit; "evil spirit" being the general term for the demon while "unclean spirit" was the description of a demon that found its element among the tombs and other places that were most unclean. The Gemmara speaks of the necromancer who visits burial places to be better inspired by an unclean spirit.[28] Similarly, they understood those with the spirit of python, or the prophesying spirit to be of the same kind. Here then is the significance of the Messiah's first recorded exorcism, that it demonstrated the power of the Messiah over Satan, especially Satan seen as the Serpent (the spirit of python),[29] and Satan as an unclean Spirit, who had the power of death and produced in humans the fear of death (Heb. 2:14-15).

It is clear that the grip of Satan on the population would have to be broken before Israel could be free to accept (or reject)

---

27   John Lightfoot, p. 76-77, 140-142.
28   Sanhedrin 65b (Babylonian Talmud).
29   cf. Acts 16:16.

Jesus as their Messiah. The ministry of exorcism, conducted by the Messiah and His disciples, was essential to accomplish this. By the end of this particular day, those possessed by demons had been healed, their devilish tormentors confessing as they were dismissed: *"You are the Christ* [Messiah], *the Son of God"* (Luke 4:41). Here is an indicator that demons were compelled to acknowledge the deity of Jesus as well as His Messianic office. These victories over demons were consequent upon the successful stand taken by Jesus in the wilderness, from which He had returned *"in the power of the Spirit"*.

The gospels also mention individual exorcisms, such as the Gadarene demoniac; and Mary, who had been possessed by seven devils. The one in Luke 4 we have already noted, and then there will be the very important case in Matthew 12 when the Sanhedrists charged Jesus of being a servant to Beelzebub.

Jesus delegated this power over Satan's domain to His disciples when He sent them out to the towns and villages of Israel: *"Behold, I give you the authority to trample on serpents and scorpions, and over all the power of the enemy, and nothing shall by any means hurt you"* (Luke 10:19). They exercised this power in the name of the Messiah (v. 17). Matthew described the power delegated to the twelve apostles: *"And as you go, preach, saying, The kingdom of heaven is at hand. Heal the sick, cleanse the lepers, raise the dead, cast out demons. Freely you have received, freely give"* (Matt. 10:7). The early Church continued this ministry (Acts 8:7; 16:18; 19:12).

The Second Attesting Sign: Mastery Over Leprosy

The healing of leprosy as a Messianic sign was of fundamental importance to the Jewish people, because:

1. It was a visual of the judgment of God on sin,
2. It had been an attesting sign for Moses, and
3. The Law of Moses had a prescribed ritual for the atonement of a cleansed leper.

Remarkably, there is no record in the T'nach of any individual healed of the living death under the Mosaic Law. Some argue from the silence of Scripture that the priests never once performed the cleansing rite of Leviticus 14. If Jesus could heal leprosy, it could be the single most powerful evidence of His Messianic credentials.

The case of the leper was dire. The isolation imposed on him not only took him out of any social contact with others, but also removed him from any support the Temple and its sacrifices might give. Rabbinism confessed itself powerless in the presence of this living death.

If the first attesting sign (the healing of those demon possessed) is prominent in Luke 4, then the second attesting sign (the healing of leprosy) is prominent in Luke 5. *"Behold, a man who was full of leprosy saw Jesus; and he fell on his face and implored Him, saying, 'Lord, if You are willing, You can make me clean.' Then He* [Jesus] *put out His hand and touched him, saying, 'I am willing; be cleansed.' Immediately the leprosy left him"* (Luke 5:12-13). It is significant that this first recorded case of leprosy treated by the Messiah was a person *"full of leprosy"*. The disease had such a hold that it had almost extinguished life. It had run its course and had the decaying man firmly in its grip. Since leprosy is called the "living death" and is, according to the Mishnah, a "father of uncleanness", and is listed next to "corpse uncleanness"[30], how remarkable is the action of the Messiah, *"He put out His hand and touched him"* (v. 13). The creeping death fled before the Lord of life. The touch of *"the resurrection and the life"* (John 11:25) regenerated the dying body of the diseased man. Jesus instructed the leper to report to the priest, and offer those sacrifices that were required by the law.

The ministry to lepers does not have as much prominence in the gospels as the ministry of exorcisms. Nevertheless, there are those touches to show that it was an integral part of the overall mission of the Messiah. When John sent to Jesus for confirmation of His Messiahship, the Messiah offered His miraculous ministry as proof. Included in the catalogue of attesting signs was the ministry to lepers. *"Jesus answered and said to them, 'Go and tell John the things that you hear and see: The blind see and the lame walk; the lepers are cleansed and the deaf hear; the dead are raised up and the poor have the gospel preached to them'"* (Matt. 11:4-5). Observe

---

30   Kelim 1.1 (Mishnah).

again that Jesus used the word "cleansed", not healed.

The most prominent case is the incident when the Messiah, having been rejected, sent ten healed lepers to the Temple to demonstrate this Messianic sign in all its fullness. The ten (a significant number) were healed together, healed from a distance and healed completely. Jesus demonstrated to the Sanhedrin in no uncertain terms, that He was truly their Messiah and that they had made a terrible mistake.

Like the casting out of demons, Jesus also delegated this ministry to the apostles, to offer further proof to the nation that He was truly Israel's Messiah (Matt. 10:8).

The Third Attesting Sign: Water into Blood

In the case of Moses, the first two attesting signs were performed immediately at the bush, but the third attesting sign was not used until he had travelled back to Egypt. Similarly, in the ministry of the Messiah, the first two signs have early prominence, but the third sign does not feature until the conclusion of His ministry and life. We need to wait a little before examining the purpose of this third element of the attestation of the Messiah. It will occupy our attention in chapter ten.

Other Attesting Signs

As Moses performed other miracles so too did Jesus. His were performed, (i) for the population generally, (ii) for disciples and (iii) for individuals. There was deliverance for those who were "bound by Satan", the most prominent of which we will examine later. But there are two groups of miracles that deserve special mention—the healing of those who were blind and the raising of the dead. Light and life are the twin motifs of John's gospel, and to support them there is the healing of the blind man and the raising of Lazarus. In the synoptics the examples are multiplied.

Giving Sight to the Blind

As previously intimated, Jesus included the healing of the blind in His catalogue of miracles that was evidence of His Messiahship (Matt. 11:5). He also inserted the healing of the blind into the Messianic passage that He quoted from Isaiah 61:1-2. In Isaiah it reads:

> *The Spirit of the Lord God is upon Me,*
> *Because the Lord has anointed Me*
> *To preach good tidings to the poor;*
> *He has sent Me to heal the broken-hearted,*
> *To proclaim liberty to the captives,*
> *And the opening of the prison to those who are bound;*
> *To proclaim the acceptable year of the Lord.*

Whereas Jesus said,

> *The Spirit of the Lord is upon Me,*
> *Because He has anointed Me*
> *To preach the gospel to the poor;*
> *He has sent Me to heal the broken-hearted,*
> *To proclaim liberty to the captives*
> *And recovery of sight to the blind,*
> *To set at liberty those who are oppressed,*
> *To proclaim the acceptable year of the Lord* (Luke 4:18).

Multiple healings of the blind were among His Messianic signs. *"Great multitudes came to Him, having with them the lame, blind, mute, maimed, and many others; and they laid them down at Jesus' feet, and He healed them. So the multitude marvelled when they saw the mute speaking, the maimed made whole, the lame walking, and the blind seeing; and they glorified the God of Israel"* (Matt. 15:29-31), and *"Then the blind and the lame came to Him in the temple, and He healed them"* (Matt. 21:14).

Then there were specific healings that one or more of the synoptic writers recorded for us. They are:

- Two blind men healed together, before the Messiah's rejection (Matt. 20:29-33),
- A blind, demon-possessed man—this was a Pharisaical test of His Messiahship (Matt. 12:22).
- Two blind men healed together, after the Messiah's rejection (Matt. 20:30-33; Mark 10:46-52; Luke 18:35-43).
- A blind man healed in two stages (Mark 8:22-26).

On most occasions, Jesus touched their eyes and they received sight. However, Mark recorded an incident when Jesus took a blind man to a location outside the centre of population and performed the miracle in two stages. The first stage brought light without clarity. A further touch of the Messiah completed the healing. In some ways, it was an illustration of what was happening in the personal experience of many who heard Him.

Israel's Messiah received great opposition from the ruling classes. Jesus called them thieves, robbers and fools. One of His most used epithets was "blind". They were *"blind leaders of the blind"* (Matt. 15:14). *"Woe to you, blind guides … fools and blind… fools and blind…blind guides…blind Pharisee"* (Matt. 23:16-26). The Pharisees, protectors of the traditions of the elders, believed they had the most light. They were the ones to lead Israel into the good graces of God via the paths of Pharisaic righteousness. Jesus Messiah advised the population not to follow them. They were blind guides, living and walking in darkness, following a path that would lead to destruction.

As the "Bread of Life", He fed the multitude with bread; as the "Resurrection and the Life", He raised the dead; but as the "Light of the World", He gave sight to the blind. The individual healings chosen by the writers of the gospels not only demonstrated the compassion and ministry of the Messiah but were also object lessons of what was occurring in the spiritual realm.

The incarnate Son of God came to give Israel sight. He offered to open their spiritual eyes, to give them light, the light of God. If they received Him as Messiah, they would receive further illumination from the Word of God. He would lift the veil from their eyes.[31] Rabbinic teaching understood Messiah's name to be "Light". The light that illuminated the hills of Bethlehem at His birth, and was seen as far away as Babylonia, was emblematic of the light He offered. He would provide them with light to illuminate, to enlighten, to educate and to guide—light for the mind and light for the spirit. The Messiah, who would sit on David's throne in the Messianic kingdom, would be clothed in light as He was on the Mount of Transfiguration (Matt. 17:2).

---

31   Cf. 2 Cor. 3:13-16.

Citizens in the Messianic kingdom would bask in that light.

But the leaders said they were not blind! They asserted that they did not need their eyes to be opened—they could see very well. Therefore, Jesus left them in darkness! Their condemnation was that they loved darkness rather than light because their deeds were evil (John 3:19).

Others, by faith asked for light, like the blind men who called upon the Son of David for healing—these were granted light. For some, their early encounters with Jesus brought light without clarity. Like the blind man who was healed in two stages, they needed a second touch. Like the two on the road to Emmaus, who saw Jesus but did not recognize Him, they needed further ministry. Jews like Nicodemus, first saw Jesus as a teacher sent from God—but later came to full discernment of His Messianic office.

Perhaps the two stage healing was more pertinent to the two stage ministry of light to the nation. The first touch was symbolic of the ministry of John the Baptist. He was a *"burning and shining lamp"* and the Jews rejoiced in his light (John 5:35). But *"He was not the Light, but he came to testify about the Light"* (John 1:8 NASB). The second touch was symbolic of the ministry of the Messiah, *"the true Light"* (v. 9).

Raising the Dead

Besides healing those who were almost dead, Jesus Messiah raised those who had died. The gospel narratives record the raising of the dead in general terms. When the Messiah gave His disciples power to raise the dead (Matt. 10:8), they were able to report to John, *"the blind see and the lame walk; the lepers are cleansed and the deaf hear: the dead are raised up and the poor have the gospel preached to them"* (11:5).

The gospel writers have also included a sample selection of this particular genre of miracle. The three synoptic writers recorded the "quickening" of a young girl, the twelve-year-old daughter of Jairus, a synagogue ruler.[32] Luke added an incident when Jesus stopped a funeral to raise a widow's son (Luke 7:11 ff). In addition, John is famous for his narrative of the raising of Lazarus, beloved brother of Mary and Martha, who had been in the tomb

32   Matt. 9:18 ff; Mark 5:22 ff; Luke 8:41 ff.

four days.

A comparison of the three miracles would show :

A daughter	A son	A brother
Just died	Dead a day	Dead 4 days
In the home	At the funeral	At the cemetery
Raised from a bed	Raised from a bier	Raised from the tomb
She ate	He talked	He walked

Raising the dead was the most startling of all His miracles. To give sight to the blind was wonderful, to loosen the limbs of the paralyzed extraordinary, to cleanse a leper was amazing, to provide hearing for the deaf and speech for the dumb was remarkable, to give clarity of thought to the lunatic was astonishing, but when He raised the dead He did all these things at one time. To give life to a corpse, especially one who had been in the grave for days, was astounding. The cadaver is blind, deaf, dumb, paralyzed, numb, unclean and without a thought in its head, all combined. In giving them the essence of life he provided sight, speech, feeling, hearing, mobility and, best of all, a head full of thoughts, imaginations and aspirations—in other words, He caused them to live.

Nevertheless, it was still not the final answer, for each of these three died again, but they were tokens of an ultimate resurrection. Martha said, *"I know that he* [my brother Lazarus] *will rise again in the resurrection at the last day"* (John 11:24). The resurrection of which Martha spoke, is still future—then the dead will rise to die no more. Confidence in that resurrection is justified, because Jesus raised the dead while incarnate on earth. The second fact that gives confidence is, Jesus also rose from the dead—rose to die no more. He is the firstfruits of those who died (1 Cor. 15:20,23). In Jesus we have the answer to the question Ezekiel raised in the giant graveyard, *"Can these bones live?"* Messiah's answer is an unequivocal "Yes".

When Jesus died, He descended into Hades, and emptied that part where the Old Testament saints were resting, namely, that section of Hades called Abraham's bosom or Paradise. As a sign that this was accomplished, the Messiah sent into Jerusalem many resurrected saints after His own resurrection (Matt. 27:52). It was the sign of the prophet Jonah multiplied many times.[33]

---

33   See chapter 10.

CHAPTER 5

Authenticating Miracles in John's Gospel

Setting the Scene

The Prologue

John wrote his gospel after Matthew, Mark and Luke had completed theirs. The subject of His book is *"Jesus the Christ* [Messiah], *the Son of God"* (20:30-31). He begins with a prologue explaining the person and work of the Messiah, and initially calls Him *"the Word"*, *"o λόγος"*. John 1:1 reads, *"In the begin-ning was the Word, and the Word was with God, and the Word was God"*: *"εν αρχη ην ο λόγος, και ο λόγος ην προς τον θεόν, και θεος ην ο λόγος."*

Because the gospel was written in Greek, some commen-tators use the Greek philosophical definition of *"logos"*, that it is "reason and speech", modifying it only slightly, to explain John's use of the word. Nevertheless, John is no Greek philoso-pher. Yet he did speak Aramaic (the main language in Israel at that time) and knew of the Aramaic paraphrases of the Hebrew Scriptures that were in use in synagogues, before, during, and after, the time of the Messiah. The synagogues employed these paraphrases, called Targums, because many of the common people could not understand Hebrew. The normal practice was to read a verse from the Torah in Hebrew, and then the official translator known as the Turgeman (or Meturgeman), would give the Aramaic rendering. The Aramaic paraphrase would contain more than just the translation—it would sometimes carry a measure of amplification. The popularity of the Aramaic versions is indicated by the Rabbinic imperative to review the weekly Torah section twice from the Biblical text and once from the Targum.[34]

In the Targums, the "*Memra*" of YHWH is substituted for YHWH:[35]

(i)   where YHWH is anthropomorphisized, or
(ii) where two or more YHWHs seem to be indicated by the text,
(iii) where the immanent aspect of God is indicated, i.e. to connote the manifestation on earth and among men of several aspects of divine power such as goodness, wisdom, justice. The *Memra* is "the intersection between God's response to Israel and Israel's to God."[36]

Examples include: *"And Abraham worshipped and prayed in the name of the Memra of YHWH, and said, 'You are YHWH who does see, but You cannot be seen.'"*[37] Here, two YHWHs are apparent. Abraham prayed in the name of the *Memra* of YHWH but is praying to the YHWH who cannot be seen.

As indicated, the Targums not only paraphrased the Hebrew T'nach but also included some commentary that reflected the views of the Rabbis. John, familiar with the Targums, was also familiar with their theology of the "*Memra*". Therefore, it is feasible that the Greek title "*Logos*" in John's gospel is meant to convey the Aramaic "*Memra*". The Rabbis said several things in respect of the *Memra* of God.

The *Memra* is the same as God, reigning supreme upon the Almighty's throne: *"For what people so great, to whom the Lord is so high in the Name of the Memra of the Lord? ... the Memra of the Lord sits upon His throne high and lifted up, and hears our prayers what*

---

34   Berakoth 8a (Babylonian Talmud).

35   "The designation for God most characteristic of all the Targums is 'the Memra of the Lord'. This is found 314 times in Neofiti and 636 times in Neofiti marginal gloss; in Fragment Targums about 99 times; in Onqelos 178 times and 322 times in Pseudo-Jonathon" (Intro. to Targum Neofiti 1: Genesis: p. 37).

36   Bruce D. Chilton, <u>The Aramaic Bible—The Targums</u>. (Edinburgh: T & T Clark Ltd., 1987), Introduction to the Isaiah Targum.

37   Gen. 22:14, Targum.Neofiti 1: Genesis.

time we pray before Him and make our petitions" (Deut. 4:7). Again, Genesis 28:20-21: *"And Jacob vowed a vow, saying, 'If the Memra of* YHWH *will be my support, and will keep me in the way that I go, and will give me bread to eat, and raiment to put on, so that I come again to my father's house in peace; then shall the Memra of* YHWH *be my God.'"* Here, Jacob, Patriarch of Israel, worshipped the *Memra* as God. Then again, "the *Memra* of the Lord created man in His likeness, in the likeness of the presence of the Lord He created him, the male and his yoke-fellow He created them."[38] John echoed this in his prologue and said, *"the Word was God"* (John 1:1). The deity of Jesus is a major theme of his gospel.

The *Memra* is Distinct from God. For example, in Genesis 19:24, the T'nach says, *"Then the Lord* [YHWH] *rained brimstone and fire on Sodom and Gomorrah, from the Lord* [YHWH] *out of the heavens."* In Hebrew, the grammar indicates that one YHWH rains fire from another YHWH, so the Targum Jonathan reads, *"And the Memra* [Word] *of the* YHWH *caused to descend upon the peoples of Sodom and Gommorah, brimstone and fire from the* YHWH *in heaven."* John, while saying Jesus Messiah is the same as God also says He is distinct from God. *"The Word was with God"* (1:1).

The *Memra* is the Agent of Creation. *"By the Memra of* YHWH *were the heavens made; and all the hosts of them by the Spirit of his mouth"* (Ps. 33:6). *"From the beginning with wisdom the Memra of the Lord created and perfected the heavens and the earth"* (Gen. 1:1). It was used in the Aramaic translation of the Old Testament. There is an example in Isaiah 45:12: *"I have made the earth, and created man on it."* In the Aramaic it is, *"I, by my word* [Memra]*, have made...."*; then again, Isaiah 48:13, *"My hand has laid the foundation of the earth."* In the Aramaic it reads, *"by my word* [Memra] *I have founded the earth."* John says of Jesus, *"All things were made through Him, and without Him nothing was made that was made"* (John 1:3). Again, *"He was in the world, and the world was made through Him, and the world did not know Him"* (v. 10).

The *Memra* is the agent of revelation. Moses wrote, *"The word* [Memra] *of the Lord came to Abram in a vision saying..."* (Gen. 15:4). On this occasion the Lord declared, *"My Memra shall be your strength, your reward shall be very great."*[39] Abram's response

38   Gen. 1:27, Targum.Neofiti 1: Genesis.
39   Gen. 15:1, Targum Onqelos.

was to ask for an heir, so he is given further revelation. *"The word* [Memra] *of the Lord came* to *him saying...."* (Gen. 15:4). This further revelation was to promise a son through whom would come a great nation. The New King James Bible translates verse 6, *"And he believed in the Lord, and He accounted it to him for righteousness"*, whereas the Targum Neofiti 1 reads, *"and Abram believed in the name of the Memra of the Lord and it was reckoned to him as righteousness"* (cf. Rom. 4:3). John wrote, *"No one has seen God at any time. The only begotten Son, who is in the bosom of the Father, He has declared Him"* (John 1:18). In John's writings Jesus (the *Memra*) is the agent of revelation, described in terms of light and truth. He is, *"the true Light which, coming into the world, enlightens every man"* (1:9 NASB).

The *Memra* is the Agent of Salvation. In the section in Exodus where God has come down to deliver, the Jerusalem Targum adds to the aspect of creation by the *Memra* this aspect of salvation by the *Memra. "And the Memra of* YHWH *said to Moses, 'I am He who said unto the world "Be!" and it was: and who in the future shall say to it "Be!" and it shall be.' And He said, 'Thus you shall say to the children of Israel:* I AM *has sent me to you.'"*[40] Note that the *Memra* is the I AM of Exodus, which is of particular significance to John. Then again, verses in the prophets speak of salvation, for example, *"Israel shall be saved by the Lord with an everlasting salvation"* (Isa. 45:17). The Targum Jonathan puts it, *"Israel will be redeemed by the Memra of God, an everlasting redemption."* Again, *"Look to Me, and be saved, All you ends of the earth! For I am God, and there is no other"*, which the Targum puts, *"Turn to my Memra all dwellers on earth. I am the* LORD, *there is no other"* (v. 22). In Hosea, *"I will have pity on the people of the house of Judah, and I will save them by the Memra of* YHWH, *their God."*[41] John says of Jesus, *"But as many as received Him, to them He gave the right to become children of God, to those who believe in His name"* (John 1:12).

The *Memra* is the means by which God became visible—the Shekinah. The Shekinah is the visible manifestation of the presence of God by light, fire or cloud (or a combination of any or all). For example, at the burning bush, "the *Memra* of YHWH" spoke to Moses. Another example would be, *"When the ark came*

40   Ex. 3:14, Jerusalem Targum.
41   Hos. 1:7, "The Targum of the Minor Prophets".

to a stop the cloud surrounded them…And Moses stood in prayer and asked mercy from God and said, 'Do good to us as the Memra of God with your mercy for thy nation of Israel. And blessed is the Shekinah among them…'[42] John said, "The Word [*Memra*] *was made flesh, and dwelt* [tabernacled, *Shekinah'd*] *among us, (and we beheld his glory, the glory as of the only begotten of the Father,) full of grace and truth"* (John 1:14).

The *Memra* is the Mediator of the covenants of the T'nach. For example, Noah's Covenant: *"And* YHWH *said to Noah, This is the sign of the covenant which I have established between My Memra and* [between] *all flesh that is upon the earth."*[43] In addition, the Abrahamic Covenant: *"I will establish My covenant between My Memra and* [between] *you and* [between] *your children after you, throughout their generations, as an eternal covenant to be God to you and to your children after you."*[44] The Rabbis taught that the *Memra* established the Mosaic covenant. John says that the covenant of grace is similarly authorized: *"For the law was given through Moses,* [signed by the Shekinah] *but grace and truth came through Jesus Christ"* (John 1:17).

In summary, those that interpret "the Word", mentioned in the prologue to John's gospel, in terms of reason and speech, or debate the finer points of *"logos"* and *"rhema"* (simply because the gospel was written in the Greek language) miss the fact that Christianity was born in a Jewish context amidst Jewish teaching. John was finding a way to demonstrate that the *Memra*, whom the Jewish nation accepted as God, obeyed as God, and worshipped as God, was Jesus of Nazareth, the rejected Messiah. He was, in fact, another and more perfect Shekinah manifestation, who came to inaugurate the promised New Covenant.

Jesus the *Logos*, the *Memra*, the Word, is:
1. Distinct from God;
2. The same as God;
3. The agent of creation;
4. The agent of revelation;
5. The agent of salvation;

---

42   Num. 10:36, Targum Jonathan.
43   Gen. 9:17, Targum Onqelos.
44   Gen. 17:7, Targum Onqelos.

6.   A visible manifestation of God; and
7.   Mediator of the New Covenant.

John's prologue (vv. 1-18) establishes each of these points:

"In the beginning was the Word, and the Word was with God, (that is, (1) distinct from God) *and the Word was God.* (That is, (2) the same as God.)

He was in the beginning with God. (That is, (1) distinct from God.)

All things were made through Him, and without Him nothing was made that was made. (That is, (3) the agent of creation.)

In Him was life, and the life was the light of men. And the light shines in the darkness, and the darkness did not comprehend it...That was the true Light which gives light to every man coming into the world. (That is, (4) the agent of revelation.)

He was in the world, and the world was made through Him, (that is, (3) the agent of creation) *and the world did not know Him. He came to His own, and His own did not receive Him.*

But as many as received Him, to them He gave the right to become children of God, to those who believe in His name: who were born, not of blood, nor of the will of the flesh, nor of the will of man, but of God. (That is, (5) the agent of salvation.)

And the Word became flesh and dwelt among us, and we beheld His glory, the glory as of the only begotten of the Father, full of grace and truth...(That is, (6) a visible manifestation of God.)

For the law was given through Moses, but grace and truth came through Jesus Christ." (That is, (7) mediator of the New Covenant.)

While John began with a prologue explaining the person and work of Jesus, (the Word, the *Memra*, the Messiah), his final summary statement contains his reasons for selecting the miracles included in his gospel biography. He wrote, *"These miracles* [signs] *are written that you may believe that Jesus is the Christ* [Messiah], *the Son of God, and that believing you may have life in His name"* (20:30-31). His record of the miracles was designed to illustrate what it was like to have the *Memra* of God, the divine agent of creation, revelation, and salvation walking among men as Messiah.

The Sign for the Forerunner of the Messiah

Before looking at the miracles (signs) in John's gospel, it is appropriate to pause for a moment and look at the sign from heaven that identified Jesus as the Son of God. Before Jesus started His public ministry, John the Baptist had a remarkable experience. He spoke of it. *"I saw the Spirit descending from heaven like a dove, and He remained upon Him. I did not know Him, but He who sent me to baptize with water said to me, 'Upon whom you see the Spirit descending, and remaining on Him, this is He who baptizes with the Holy Spirit.' And I have seen and testified that this is the Son of God"* (1:32-34). Here then is the first sign of deity. At the baptism of the Messiah, the invisible Spirit of God took physical form as a dove and rested upon Him as a sign.

We can better understand the implications of this sign when we consider it in conjunction with another event. The Temple authorities asked Jesus for a sign when He first cleansed the Temple. Having driven out the mercenary influences from the Temple area, they wanted Jesus to justify His actions, so they asked Him: *"What sign do You show to us, since You do these things?"* (John 2:18). He replied: *"Destroy this temple, and in three days I will raise it up"* (v. 19). John explained that He was speaking of His body not the Jewish second temple. Here Jesus is already intimating the sign that will occupy our attention later, that of the prophet Jonah: *"For as Jonah was three days and three nights in the belly of the great fish, so will the Son of Man be three days and three nights in the heart of the earth"* (Matt. 12:40 NASB). But our immediate concern is the reference to His body as the Temple.

The Temple of Solomon (as also the Tabernacle) had certain things that signified and authorized it as the place where man could meet with God. They included:

(i)   the divine presence/the divine glory
(ii) the instruments of divine guidance, the Urim and Thummim,
(iii) the anointing oil,
(iv) the ark with the mercy seat and the cherubim.

These were not present in Herod's Temple. When the destruction of Solomon's temple drew near, the divine presence went up from the propitiatory and never returned (Ezek. 10:4). The ark with the mercy seat and cherubim was lost; as was the recipe for the anointing oil. The oracle by Urim and Thummim was never restored. The Talmudists said, "Things are not asked or inquired after now (by Urim and Thummim) by the High Priest, because he does not speak by the Holy Spirit, nor does there any divine afflatus breathe on him."

Its association with the name of Herod further degraded the Temple. The Jews object: "It is not permitted to anyone to demolish one synagogue, till he has built another." Therefore, it was much more heinous to demolish the Temple; but Herod ignored such concerns and demolished the Temple before rebuilding it.

The sign to the Baptist and the statement of the Messiah when taken together, declare that the building, (i) which bore the unholy name of Herod, (ii) which was governed by a band of thieves, and (iii) was home to those who opposed God's true Messiah, could not be the true Temple of God.

On the other hand,

(i)   Jesus the Messiah, was graced with the divine presence as the Bat Qols[45] testify, and although for the most part the divine glory was veiled there was a night when a mountain top was lit up by a light brighter than the noon-day sun (Matt. 17:2).

(ii) Because He had access to the divine presence, He had divine guidance better than that which was available through the use of the Urim and Thummim.

(iii) Furthermore, His title Messiah, which means "Anointed", required Him to be anointed to fulfil His office. This anointing took place on the bank of Jordan when the Spirit of God descended and rested upon Him (Matt. 3:16). Jesus would also be the One to pour out the Spirit at the Feast of Pentecost after His ascension (Acts 2:33).

(iv) Jesus Messiah is also our propitiatory. *"Τω ἱλαστήριον"*

---

45   Matt. 3:17; 17:5-6; Mark 1:11; John 12:28.

(*hilastērion*) refers to the "mercy seat" in the Sanctuary (Heb. 9:5). A similar word is used of the Messiah. John the Apostle wrote, "*Jesus Christ the righteous...is the propitiation* ['ίλασμός' (*hilasmos*)] *for our sins, and not for ours only but also for the whole world*" (1 Jn. 2:2). And again, "*In this is love, not that we loved God, but that He loved us and sent His Son to be the propitiation* ['ίλασμός' (*hilasmos*)] *for our sins*" (4:10). He is our propitiatory. Not only so, but the mercy seat was protected by angelic guardians. So also the Messiah, especially at those times when He was most vulnerable to attacks from the Evil One. [46]

In other words, the real Temple of God, where God can truly meet with man, which has the Shekinah Glory, the Holy Spirit, the propitiatory, the oracle of the Urim and Thummin, the protecting cherubim and the anointing oil, is the body of Christ, identified to the Baptist by the Father.

---

46   Matt. 1:24; 2:13,19-20; 4:11; 26:53; Mark 1:13; Luke 22:43.

CHAPTER 6
Authenticating Miracles in John's Gospel: The Attesting Signs

While the attesting miracles in John are recorded that the "whoever" might believe, they each have significance, either for the nation or the disciples, and sometimes for both. There are 17 references using the word "σημεῖον" (*semeion*) in John's gospel—in the NKJV translated "sign" each time. [47]

John listed and described the attesting miracles so that the readers might believe (20:30). Therefore, it is interesting to note that the miracle signs did not always accomplish that purpose when performed in the presence of others. John's first reference that includes the word *"semeion"* is 2:11; *"This beginning of signs Jesus did in Cana of Galilee, and manifested His glory; and His disciples believed in Him."* Here, the sign for His disciples accomplished the stated purpose, *"His disciples believed in Him."* The last verse that includes the *"semeion"* (apart from the summary text) is 12:37, *"But although He had done so many signs before them, they did not believe in Him."* Here, the signs for the general population and especially for the leadership did not accomplish the designed objective. *"He came to His own, and His own did not receive Him. But as many as received Him, to them He gave the right to become children of God, to those who believe in His name"* (John 1:11-12). These texts encapsulate two of the main points—there was more than enough evidence for the nation to believe—so many signs—but only a remnant did.

Now let us consider the miracles (signs) as recorded by

---

47   John 2:11,18,23; 3:2; 4:48,54; 6:2,14,26,30; 7:31; 9:16; 10:41; 11:47; 12:18,37.

John. They are:

1. Changing water into wine
2. Healing a ruler's son
3. Healing a disabled man
4. Feeding a large crowd
5. Walking on the sea
6. Healing the man born blind
7. Raising a dead man
8. The miraculous catch of fish

The First of the Significant Miracles in John: Changing Water into Wine

John identifies the miracle at the wedding in Cana of Galilee as being the first (2:1-11). Nevertheless, it appears from the words of the Messiah that it is out of chronological order. The grace of God permits it, but the real significance of the miracle applies to the end of His life. This is why He said to His mother, *"My hour has not yet come"* (v. 4).

The main facts are these. Jesus and His disciples attended a wedding where they ran out of wine. When His mother brought this information to His attention, she expected Him to do something about it. He commandeered the six giant water pots that held water for the ritual cleansing of the family and guests. Each of the water pots held between twenty and thirty gallons. The Messiah ordered the servants to fill them with water. The servants filled them to the brim. He changed this water into wine— the best wine, according to the governor of the celebrations. John adds, *"This beginning of signs Jesus did in Cana of Galilee, and manifested His glory; and His disciples believed in Him"* (v. 11).

This first miracle demonstrates the seeds of the move from law to grace. John had previously stated, *"The law was given through Moses, but grace and truth came through Jesus Christ."* (1:17). The water, which had been set aside for the rituals of purification, is a reminder of the legal requirements imposed on the population at that time. The Pharisees wanted the general population to observe the rules of purification that the priests in the Temple obeyed. They were aiming to establish a kingdom of priests! These champions of legalism were legislating joy out of the nation. Jesus turned the water, symbolic of the ritual cleansing under the Mosaic covenant, into wine, the symbol both of the New Covenant (Luke 22:20), where it represents the blood of the Messiah shed for sin, and the blessing under the Melchizedekian priesthood (Gen. 14:18). In providing between 120 and 180 gallons of the best wine it is also a physical illustration of the text, *"I am come that they might have life and that they may have it more abundantly"* (John 10:10).

At a wedding feast, they formally drank several cups of wine. The first was the cup of Terumah, which denoted that the virgin bride might have had a priest as a bridegroom. (The Church's bridegroom will be the High Priest of the order of Melchizedek[48]). The second cup was the cup of good news when they proclaimed and certified the virginity of the bride. (The Church is espoused to Christ as a chaste virgin[49]). They pronounced the bridegroom's blessing over the third cup: a blessing that was repeated every day of the feast.

At this wedding attended by Jesus and His disciples, the supply of wine ran dry. Mary asked her son to address the problem. Jesus, as Messiah of Israel, rather than Mary's son, responded to the challenge.

It is unlikely the wine ran out before they drank the cup of Terumah, because that took place at the beginning of the celebrations. For the same reason, it is unlikely, that it was before the cup of good news. It could be that the problem surfaced when the governor of the feast was preparing to pronounce another of the bridegroom's blessings, or perhaps a blessing after the order of the customary sevenfold marriage blessing.[50]

Nowadays, the sevenfold marriage blessing is:

1. You abound in blessings, Adonai our God, who created the fruit of the vine.
2. You abound in blessings, Adonai our God, You created all things for Your glory.

---

48   Heb. 6:20.
49   2 Cor. 11:2.
50   Scott-Martin Kosofsky, <u>Book of Customs: A Complete Handbook for the Jewish Year</u>. (San Francisco: Harper, 2004) p. 370-371.

3. You abound in blessings, Adonai our God, You created humanity.
4. You abound in blessings, Adonai our God, You made humankind in Your image, after Your likeness, and you prepared for us a perpetual relationship. You abound in blessings, Adonai our God, you created humanity.
5. May she who was barren rejoice when her children are united in her midst in joy. You abound in blessings, Adonai our God, who makes Zion rejoice with her children.
6. You make these beloved companions greatly rejoice even as You rejoiced in Your creation in the Garden of Eden as of old. You abound in blessings, Adonai our God, who makes the bridegroom and bride to rejoice.
7. You abound in blessings, Adonai our God, who created joy and gladness, bridegroom and bride, mirth and exultation, pleasure and delight, love, fellowship, peace and friendship. Soon may there be heard in the cities of Judah and in the streets of Jerusalem, the voice of joy and gladness, the voice of the bridegroom and the voice of the bride, the jubilant voice of bridegrooms from their canopies and of youths from their feasts of song. You abound in blessings, Adonai our God, You make the bridegroom rejoice with the bride.

For blessings of joy very similar to these, Jesus provided the wine. The One who was present in Cana was the Creator the fruit of the vine (blessing No. 1), and created all things for His glory (blessing No. 2). He created man (blessing No. 3) in His likeness, and for a relationship (blessing No. 4). He had rejoiced with Adam and Eve in Eden (blessing No. 6), and wished to bless Zion (blessing No. 5 & 7). If they would receive Him they would have joy "up to the brim" — new wine!

The suggestion, that the symbolism of the provision of wine had more to do with the end of His ministry than the beginning, gains strength, when the wine that was drunk at the Passover meal is considered. As at the wedding, wine plays a significant part in the symbolism of Passover. Even the poorest Israelite must drink at least four cups of wine.[51] Jesus's last meal before His execution was the Passover celebration. The first cup of wine at that meal had a double blessing pronounced over it. The house of Hillel says, "He (the governor of the feast) says a blessing over the wine, and afterward he says a blessing over the day."[52] The House of Shammai says, "He says a blessing over the day, and afterward he says a blessing over the wine."[53] The blessing over the wine was the same as that pronounced at the wedding. When they drank the second cup of wine, the governor of the feast would recount the reasons for the celebration of Passover.[54] The Passover meal itself, which included the roast lamb, was followed with a third cup of wine, the "cup of blessing".[55] This cup, *"the cup after supper"*, *"the cup of blessing which we bless"* (1 Cor. 10:16), is the one over which Jesus Messiah pronounced the words, *"this cup is the new covenant in My blood, which is shed for you"* (Luke 22:20). At the drinking of the fourth cup they completed the singing of the Hallel.[56] Matthew and Mark record: *"After singing a hymn, they went out to the Mount of Olives"* (Matt. 26:30; Mark 14:26). Thus,

(i) Jesus began the celebration with the joy of thanksgiving with the first cup, "the cup of thanksgiving".

(ii) In connection with the drinking of the second cup, "the cup of redemption" He recounted YHWH's grace in redeeming Israel from bondage.

(iii) The significance of the third cup, "the cup of blessing" was redefined and given a new name, "the cup of the new covenant".

(iv) Jesus concluded the feast in the customary way. He drank the fourth cup, "the cup of praise", and sang the final part of the Hallel.

These cups were "mixed"[57], that is, they contained both

---

51   Pesahim 10.1.C (Mishnah).
52   Pesahim 10.2.I.C (Mishnah).
53   Pesahim 10.2.I.B (Mishnah).
54   Pesahim 10.4.II (Mishnah).
55   Pesahim 10.7.III (Mishnah).
56   Pesahim 10.7.IV (Mishnah).
57   Pesahim 10.4.I; 10.4.II; 10.7.III (Mishnah).

wine and water, which adds further significance to the sacrifice of the Messiah upon the cross, when *"blood and water"* poured from His side (John 19:34). Blood and water are the two ritual cleansing agents and were the two cleansing agents of leprosy!

The timing of this first miracle is emphasized by John as *"the third day"* (2:1). The first day of this first week recorded by John is 1:19-28; the second day introduced by the phrase, *"the next day"*, is found in verses 29-34; the third day recorded as, *"again the next day"* is found in verses 35-42; the fourth day, identified by the phrase, *"the following day"* is found in verses 43-51. It is on the third day after that, i.e. after the fourth day, that there was a marriage. At the end of the first week in Genesis, the pre-incarnate Son of God attended a marriage between Adam and Eve. At the end of the first week that John records, the incarnate Son of God also attended a marriage!

Those attending the wedding were aware of the significance given to marriage in the T'nach. It was customary, then as now, to reflect on the marriage that took place in the Garden of Eden, which God blessed by His presence. (See blessing no. 6 earlier). Jesus used this occasion to reveal Himself to His disciples as the creator God, or as John puts it, Jesus, *"manifested* [revealed] *His glory"* (2:11), that is made visible and known, the glory of God incarnate. "Manifested" or "revealed" is a word to indicate a revelation—something hidden, now visible. It is the word that Jesus used in His high priestly prayer, when He asserted that He had disclosed to them the divine reality, the name of God, *"I have manifested Your name to the men whom You have given Me out of the world"* (17:6). No wonder John declared, *"The Word became flesh and dwelt among us, and we beheld His glory"* (1:14).

The Second of the Significant Miracles in John: Healing a Ruler's Son

The second sign that John records is the healing of the sick son of a royal official, a boy who was at the point of death. Jesus, located in Cana, was asked by a nobleman, to visit Capernaum to heal his son (John 4:46-54). From the narrative it appears that this father was an Herodian, not merely a servant of Herod but one devoted to his family out of principles of submission and conscience. The Greek word *basilikos* suggests a man of high standing in the court of Herod. The reply of the Messiah to the Herodian's request was: *"Unless you people see signs and wonders, you will by no means believe"* (v. 48). In this response, he was levelling a charge that not only applied to the Jews generally, but to Herod's court in particular (1 Cor 1:22). Luke tells us that Herod himself rejoiced when Pilate sent Jesus to him: *"for he had wanted to see Him for a long time, because he had been hearing about Him and was hoping to see some sign performed by Him"* (Luke 23:8 NASB). The Herodian, now a distraught father, continued to plead: *"Sir, come down before my child dies!"* to which the Messiah responded, *"Go your way; your son lives."* The word of the Lord was accepted, the son was healed from that very hour, and both the nobleman and those of his household became believers in Jesus the Messiah.

There are those that would identify this man with Chuza, the steward of Herod, whose wife became one of them that ministered of their wealth to the needs of the Messiah (Luke 8:3). Whether or not that was so, the Messianic message entered Herod's palace through this healing, and thus the sign accomplished its purpose for a family, although its effect on the court of Herod was minimal. The opposition of Herod and his followers was hard-hearted to the end. Mark recorded two later incidents. *"The Pharisees went out and immediately began conspiring with the Herodians against Him, as to how they might destroy Him"* (Mark 3:6 NASB), and *"Then they sent some of the Pharisees and Herodians to Him in order to trap Him in a statement"* (Mark 12:13 NASB). The Pharisees used the enmity of Herod as a political weapon, when they raised the question of divorce while Jesus was in his area of jurisdiction (Matt. 19:3 ff). The answer to this question got Jesus' forerunner, John, imprisoned.

Capernaum, the location of this "second" sign, was the place where Jesus made His home during the time of His public ministry. It was a place that saw many of His miracles, described by Jesus as *"mighty works"* (Matt. 11:20), and a place that received much blessing from His presence. Besides the royal official's son, He healed the centurion's servant there (Matt. 8:5 ff), the paralytic who was carried by his four friends (Matt. 9:2 ff), and Peter's mother-in-law (Matt. 8:14-15). Capernaum was one of the places where He healed *"all who were sick and those who were demon-possessed."* To emphasize the point Mark records the scene: *"The whole city was gathered at the door. Then He healed many who were sick with various diseases, and cast out many demons"* (Mark 1:32-34).

Yet, the people of Capernaum generally remained impenitent, and although privileged to see many mighty works of the Messiah, they nevertheless rejected His Messianic claim. This failure to respond to His gracious ministry brought down upon them a heavy denunciation of judgment: *"And you, Capernaum, who are exalted to heaven, will be brought down to Hades; for if the mighty works which were done in you had been done in Sodom, it would have remained until this day. But I say to you that it shall be more tolerable for the land of Sodom in the day of judgment than for you"* (Matt. 11:23-24). Signs and wonders do not guarantee faith in Jesus. The sign of the prophet Jonah will repeat this truth. In Capernaum, in miniature, was seen what would happen nationally. The generation to which Israel's Messiah came, did not believe in spite of the vast array of attesting signs, and, as a result, suffered the judgment of God.

Jesus the Messiah, in His association with Capernaum, demonstrated His exceptional knowledge of the human heart when He knew, even at an early stage, that its citizens would reject Him. Their opposition was in spite of the great swathe of miracles He performed and in spite of this extraordinary sign that He effected for a leading citizen of the town, a miracle that He executed at a distance of some miles.

His prophetic utterance not only revealed great wisdom but also hinted that He would occupy the position of "Judge of all the earth" (cf. John 5:22), and would have authority to bar obdurate unbelievers from heaven and consign them to Hades.

The Third of the Significant Miracles in John: Healing a Disabled Man

The third sign is the healing of a severely disabled man (John 5:1-16). It took place in Jerusalem, the nation's capital, at the pool of Bethesda, near the sheep gate. It was at the time of an unnamed feast. Whereas in the previous miracle those in need approached the Messiah, here with evident intent, He took the initiative. Out of the crowd at the poolside, He selected a physical wreck of a man, and asked him if he wished to be healed. The Bible tells us that the waters of Bethesda had healing virtue at certain seasons (v. 4). The *"certain seasons"* were probably feast times. So among the *"multitude of those who were sick, blind, lame, and paralyzed"* (v. 3) was this paralytic. He responded to the stranger's invitation by saying that the only resource, the healing waters, were out of his reach during the short time they were blessed. Jesus permitted no further objections and healed him with the words, *"Take up your bed and walk"* (v. 8).

Not knowing the identity of his benefactor, the now healthy Israelite climbed the Temple mount for the first time in nearly four decades, there to give thanks and praise to God for His beneficence. The merciful Messiah had given yet another person a new start, both physically and spiritually. Later that day, the One who not only had the power to loose from sin, but also to bind, found the man still in the Temple, and warned him, *"Sin no more, lest a worse thing come upon you"* (v. 14).

This sign, performed as it was in the nation's capital, has a national application. The Sanhedrin had not yet published their decision, so Jesus offers, in Jerusalem, a further pointed sign. The cure at the poolside demonstrated that the *"miqweh"*, "the immersion pool", "the fountain of living waters", "the Hope of Israel" Himself, was present to heal (Jer. 17:13-14). If they rejected Him they would be guilty of the same two sins as the generation that was taken into captivity: *"They have forsaken Me, the fountain of living waters, and hewn themselves cisterns — broken cisterns that can hold no water"* (Jer. 2:13).

The long-term invalid was a man whose condition was the result of continued sin. He had been chronically ill and disadvantaged for 38 years. This period of time reminds us of the generation which wandered in the wilderness for a further 38 years after God had found them guilty of their "stiff-necked" sin. If this sign is for the nation, then it must be a warning to those rebel leaders of the current generation. The warning to the newly invigorated man contained the pregnant phrase, *"lest a worse thing come upon you."* Later, when Jesus was accused of being demon-possessed and was formally rejected by the Sanhedrin, he told the leadership that a worse thing would come upon them. Their condition would deteriorate by a factor of seven because of their rejection of His Messianic claim (Matt. 12:45).

The emphasis here is on the matter of sin. The principles are: "the invalid is not healed until his sins are forgiven"[58] and *"Who can forgive sins, but God alone?"* (Mark 2:7; Luke 5:21). At the pool of Bethesda, served by the fountain of Siloam, Jesus brings into focus the prophecy of Zechariah: *"A fountain* [wellspring] *shall be opened for the house of David and to the inhabitants of Jerusalem for sin and for uncleanness"* (Zech. 13:1).

This healing took place on the Sabbath, and the reaction of those who had political power was to persecute Jesus and to conspire to kill Him. Their Messiah indicated that He had no alternative but to follow His mission, to obey His Father, and to heal the invalid: *"My Father has been working until now, and I have been working"* (John 5:17). The Sanhedrists were further incensed: *"Therefore the Jews sought all the more to kill Him, because He not only broke the Sabbath, but also said that God was His Father, making Himself equal with God"* (v. 18).

The Fourth of the Significant Miracles in John: Feeding a Large Crowd

The fourth miracle that John records is the feeding of the great crowd (6:5-14). It was near the feast of the Passover when Jesus decided to supply the obvious need of many thousands of people by multiplying a few loaves and a few fish. He also knew that His actions would bring the nation closer to a decision regarding His offer of the Messianic Kingdom.

The crowd, in the Messiah's eyes, was like a flock of sheep without a shepherd, and He viewed them with compassion. They had been following the old shepherds, the Sanhedrists, whom Jesus later described as wolves. Here, the Messiah presented Himself as their shepherd, in the tradition of Moses and David, former shepherds of the nation. At that time, they were between two opinions. Should they follow the old shepherds, whom Jesus described as thieves and robbers, or should they

---

58   Nedarim 41a (Babylonian Talmud); cf. Jas. 5:15.

follow the true shepherd of Israel.

The Messiah's intention was twofold. The first part concerned His identity, as He offered Himself as Messiah, the expected prophet, who like Moses would feed Israel in a wilderness; and as the son of David, the shepherd of Israel who would *"feed Jacob his people, and Israel his inheritance"* (Ps. 78:70-72 KJV).

The second element of His purpose was to provide training for His disciples who, in the course of time, would be shepherds themselves. The "shepherd in training" had first to learn that it is not the job of the sheep to find food for themselves, but the task of the shepherd to provide it for them. *"You give them something to eat"* (Matt. 14:16), is the principle. Here, away from any centres of population, there are no resources, save five loaves and two fish. But they did have the Messiah's benediction, which was enough to multiply their small repast into a giant picnic. One day, Peter and his fellow apostles would be responsible for feeding the flock. At the post-resurrection miracle, where the Lord provided bread and fish for the disciples, the Messiah commissioned Peter: *"Feed my lambs"*; *"Tend my sheep"*; *"Feed my sheep"* (John 21:15-17). The responsibility of Peter and his fellow apostles would involve them distributing what Jesus Himself provided.

The initial response to the miracle once more demonstrated John's consistent argument, that Jesus provided enough evidence to prove He was truly their Messiah. The people said: *"This is truly the Prophet who is to come into the world"* (John 6:14). They were ready there and then to take Him and make Him king, by force if necessary; but the Messiah, with His special insight into the heart of man, departed to be by Himself in the mountains.

The identity of the prophet from Nazareth continued to be the centre of debate between the people and Jesus the following day (v. 28 ff). The doctrine of the teachers of Israel at that time was a doctrine of works, so they questioned the Lord: *"What shall we do, that we might work the works of God?"* He directed them to the real issue: *"This is the work of God, that you believe in Him whom He sent."* Since they knew it was an appeal for them to accept His credentials as Messiah, true to their character, they asked for yet another miracle. They asked, *"What sign will You perform then, that we may see it and believe You? What work will You do?"* (v. 30). But the crowd had forgotten that the fathers of the wilderness generation had grumbled against God and God's Deliverer, Moses, for providing such food. The Messiah, however, had not forgotten: *"Your fathers ate the manna in the wilderness, and are dead."* There are two levels of meaning here. YHWH fed that generation of the nation miraculously, but because of their rebellion, He punished them. At one point, they were exposed to a plague of serpents. Numbers 21 has the record of the event: *"The people spoke against God and against Moses: 'Why have you brought us up out of Egypt to die in the wilderness? For there is no food and no water, and our soul loathes this worthless bread.' So the Lord sent fiery serpents among the people, and they bit the people; and many of the people of Israel died"* (vv. 5-6). The Biblical account records the physical death of the rebels, and the teaching of the Scribes at that time suggested, nay asserted, that their rebellion lost them their spiritual privileges as children of Abraham. The Mishnah states, "The generation of the wilderness has no portion in the world to come and will not stand in judgment, for it is written, *'In this wilderness they shall be consumed and there they shall die'* (Num. 14:35), the words of R. Aqiba."[59] The thrust of the argument of Jesus is that the eternal destiny of this generation is in the balance. He is offering Himself as the "Bread of Life", and those that feed on Him will live forever! He said, *"Moses did not give you the bread from heaven, but My Father gives you the true bread from heaven. For the bread of God is He who comes down from heaven and gives life to the world...I am the bread of life"* (John 6:32-35).

In this way, the Messiah incorporated into His teaching an implicit warning to the nation not to repeat the sin of the generation that came out of Egypt by rejecting the Bread of Life now offered, as well as the Father who sent Him from heaven. If Israel's leaders reject their Messiah, then judgment will fall on this generation as it did on the wilderness generation. On the other hand, those individuals who receive Jesus as Messiah will be able to feed on Him and to enjoy every aspect of abundant

---

59   Sanhedrin 10.3.V.X (Mishnah).

life. This heavenly bread will feed both mind and spirit, whereas the manna fed only the body. The manna fed the physical, not the spiritual and lasted two days at most. The life granted to those that receive Him as Messiah, would be spiritual rather than physical, eternal rather than temporal, and heavenly rather than earthly. This means they were guaranteed satisfaction and resurrection.

They rejected His offer, *"...because He said, 'I am the bread which came down from heaven.'"* Their response was: *"Is not this Jesus, the son of Joseph, whose father and mother we know?"* (vv. 41-42). Moreover, those who rejected Him were not just those who had been previously undecided. They also included those who had been His followers. This teaching even offended many of His disciples, and the Lord speaks of unbelief and betrayal among them. For Jesus knew from the beginning who they were who believed not, and who would betray Him (v. 64). *"From that time many of His disciples went back, and walked with Him no more"* (v. 66). This disloyalty was also amongst the apostles, in the person of Judas: *"Did I not choose you, the twelve, and one of you is a devil?"* (v. 70). Jesus challenged them all, *"Do you also want to go away?"* (v. 67). Peter, speaking for the eleven, responded, *"Lord, to whom shall we go? You have the words of eternal life. Also we have come to believe and know that You are the Christ, the Son of the living God"* (vv. 68-69). This small band of men, therefore, represent the faithful remnant.

The feeding of the multitude showed Jesus as the incarnate God, who came from heaven. He alone was able to say, *"He who comes to Me shall never hunger, and he who believes in Me shall never thirst...For I have come down from heaven, not to do My own will, but the will of Him who sent Me. This is the will of the Father who sent Me, that of all He has given Me I should lose nothing, but should raise it up at the last day"* (vv. 35-39).

This event encapsulated the problem He faced. Because of this miracle, the crowd, impressed by the creative power of Jesus, wanted to make Him king, but on their own terms. He did not fulfil their hopes in the way they expected. He "departed" from them (v. 15), physically illustrating the movement of the Messiah away from unbelieving Israel.

The Fifth of the Significant Miracles in John: Walking on the Sea

The fifth significant miracle was that which took place on the Sea of Galilee at night (John 6:16-21). If the storm on the lake, as some of the old commentators suggest, was Satanic in origin, then here is another example of a challenge to the Messiah. Certainly, the sea in Scripture is connected typically with the abyss, the temporary place of confinement of demons. For example, the demons in Legion, the Gadarene, referred to it in their appeal to Messiah, *"...they begged Him that He would not command them to go out into the abyss"* (Luke 8:31 NASB). Yet in that incident, although we have no indication of the ultimate intention of Jesus, they ended up in a watery prison. David, in considerable trouble, used the image of sinking into deep waters to describe his experience, *"Save me, O God; for the waters are come in unto my soul. I sink in deep mire, where there is no standing: I am come into deep waters, where the floods overflow me...Let not the waterflood overflow me, neither let the deep swallow me up, and let not the pit shut her mouth upon me"* (Ps. 69:1-2,15 KJV). On the restless sea, there is no place to stand, — and because of our sins we will be engulfed. "The devil will drag you under" is the line from an old song. Jesus was different. The sinless, spotless, Son of God walked on water. Moreover, He would not allow Satan to destroy His disciples: *"Simon, Simon, listen! Satan has demanded to sift all of you like wheat, but I have prayed for you"* (Luke 22:31 NRSV). Moreover, when He entered the boat it was immediately at its destination! Satan could neither divert the Messiah by offering Him the kingdom again, nor could he remove those disciples whom He had taken under His care; *"Of those whom You gave me I have lost none"* (John 18:9). The exception listed in Scripture is Judas, the son of perdition, who at that time was demon-possessed (6:70), and later became Satan-possessed (Luke 22:3; John 13:27).

In the miracle on the Sea of Galilee, the divine Son of God demonstrated again that He would thwart every attempt by Satan to drag Him down. The Devil, by threatening the lives of the disciples, was making a two-pronged attack. First, he tried to destroy the remnant that believed in Jesus as Messiah; and then, by the act of putting the lives of the disciples in jeopardy, he intended to lure Jesus on to the element most under his control, and most likely to accomplish his diabolical aim of bringing the Messiah down. Perhaps Satan, familiar with David's prophetic prayer, hoped to bring Jesus to the need to pray it Himself: *"Save me, O God, for the waters have threatened my life. I have sunk in deep mire, and there is no foothold; I have come into deep waters, and a flood overflows me"* (Ps. 69:1-2 NASB).

Not only did Jesus walk on water, but He also stilled the storm, saved Peter from sinking beneath the waves, and brought the craft safely home. The multitude fed, Peter saved, the devil defeated, no wonder they, *"worshipped Him, saying, 'You are certainly God's Son'"* (Matt. 14:33 NASB).

Nevertheless, it cannot be overlooked that the Messiah, in becoming a sin offering on Calvary, fully experienced all that David described: *"I sink in deep mire, where there is no standing: I am come into deep waters, where the floods overflow me."*

The Sixth of the Significant Miracles in John: Healing the Man Born Blind

This sixth significant miracle takes place on the Sabbath at the end of the feast of Tabernacles (John 9:1-41). The Messiah and His disciples had entered the Temple Mount when they saw a man with congenital blindness. They were aware of the theology of the Rabbis who taught that being born blind was the judgment of God on the individual. They claimed that this man's condition was the result of personal sin, either his own or his parents. The disciples asked: *"Rabbi, who sinned, this man, or his parents, that he was born blind?"* (v. 2). The sin of the parents as the source of the judgment was based on verses from the Pentateuch, for example: *"The Lord God...who keeps loving-kindness for thousands, who forgives iniquity, transgression and sin; yet He will by no means leave the guilty unpunished, visiting the iniquity of fathers on the children and on the grandchildren to the third and fourth generations"* (Ex. 34:6-7 NASB), and *"The Lord is slow to anger and abundant in loving-kindness, forgiving iniquity and transgression; but He will by no means clear the guilty, visiting the iniquity of the fathers on the children to the third and the fourth generations"* (Num. 14:18 NASB).

The Pharisees also taught that an individual had a good inclination and an evil inclination,[60] and that if the evil inclination had predominance in the womb, then it would be possible for the child to be born disadvantaged because of the judgment of God. The Rabbis further taught that since the infirmity was a judgment from God, only Messiah would be able to cure it. Jesus responded to the disciples' question with the assertion that the man's blindness was not the result of a judgment on personal sin. God did not inflict blindness on this individual, but rather the opposite, he would be healed, to the glory of God.

For the blind man, the Messiah made a clay poultice out of dust and spit, and applied it to his eyes. He then instructed him to go to the pool of Siloam and wash away the mudpack. When he washed, he was able to see clearly. The two ingredients of the poultice were dust and spittle. Biblically, dust represents the Adamic man (Gen. 2:7; 3:19), and to spit upon a man is to humiliate him, to count him worthless, and to consider him unworthy of the courtesies of life. This was the condition of the blind beggar. Pharisaism counted him inconsequential. On the other hand, the means of his cure, water from the pool of Siloam, symbolically represented the Spirit of God. This symbolism was at the heart of the ceremonies that took place during the week of the festival.

The Ceremony of the Pouring Out of the Waters

The Jewish nation believed that God had placed high honour upon the water of the fountain of Siloam, and consequently, on the pools of Bethesda and Siloam, which were fed from that fountain. They applied the words of the prophet to the waters, *"Therefore with joy you will draw water from the wells of salvation. For great is the Holy One of Israel in your midst"* (Isa. 12:3,6). Furthermore, they asserted, "from thence they drew the Holy Ghost."[61] This, of course, is a reference to the ceremony of the pouring out of the waters at the feast of Tabernacles. On the feast days, a priest carrying a golden pitcher would collect 6 or 7 pints of

60   cf. Berakhot 9.5.A (Mishnah).
61   Jerusalem (Palestinian) Talmud in Succah.

water from the pool of Siloam and lead a procession back to the Temple. On the way, they would sing the Psalms of Ascent[62] arriving at the court of priests at the close of the morning service. A threefold blast on the trumpets would welcome the bearer of the golden pitcher as he entered through the water gate, where another priest bearing a pitcher of wine for the drink offering joined him. The two priests ascended the rise of the altar, one going left and the other right, to pour out the libations, through funnels, to the foot of the altar. Immediately after, they sang the great "Hallel" with responses from the people. They ended by singing:

> Open to me the gates of righteousness;
> I will go through them,
> And I will praise the Lord.
> This is the gate of the Lord,
> Through which the righteous shall enter.
> I will praise You, For You have answered me,
> And have become my salvation.
> The stone which the builders rejected
> Has become the chief cornerstone.
> This was the Lord's doing;
> It is marvelous in our eyes.
> This is the day the Lord has made;
> We will rejoice and be glad in it.
> Save now, I pray, O Lord;
> O Lord, I pray, send now prosperity.
> Blessed is he who comes in the name of the Lord!
> We have blessed you from the house of the Lord.
> God is the Lord,
> And He has given us light;
> Bind the sacrifice with cords to the horns of the altar.
> You are my God, and I will praise You;
> You are my God, I will exalt You.
> Oh, give thanks to the Lord, for He is good!
> For His mercy endures forever" (Ps. 118:20-29).

Jesus, attending the ceremony at the festival, would have been intensely aware of the significance of these verses. After the ceremony of the pouring out of those waters, He proclaimed

62   Psalms 120-134.

in a loud clear voice, *"If anyone thirsts, let him come to Me and drink. He who believes in Me, as the Scripture has said, out of his heart will flow rivers of living water."* John added the explanation, *"This He spoke concerning the Spirit, whom those believing in Him would receive; for the Holy Spirit was not yet given, because Jesus was not yet glorified"* (John 7:37-39). Here Jesus claimed to be the promised *"Nabhi"*, the Prophet, the "weller-forth", the expected One. Those that exercised faith in Him would be like the pool of Siloam, reservoirs of living water out of which are drawn water libations for YHWH. God would quench their thirst and make them a blessing to others. The apostles were the best illustration of the fulfilment of this promise, since their post-Pentecost ministry was attended by conversions and miracles.

This then, is the context of the action of the Messiah in the healing of the man with congenital blindness. The stigma that had been heaped upon the man by the Pharisaic system (where sin is marked, identified and catalogued) was washed away by the Spirit of God. Jesus drew a straight line from the symbolism of the ceremony of the pouring out of the waters to the healing of the man and His office as Messiah.

The Ceremony of the Kindling of the Lamps

Furthermore, He used the other ceremony of the feast, the lighting of the menorahs,[63] to illustrate again His office and ministry. There were four menorahs, one in each corner of the court of prayer. They were 86 feet (26 meters) high, and youths of priestly descent would climb ladders to fill each of them with oil (more than 30 gallons (113 litres) each). Worn out garments of the priests had been reformed to make the wicks. At night, the menorahs were lit and the court of prayer was illuminated so brightly that its light was seen throughout Jerusalem.

This light symbolized the Shekinah that once filled the Temple, and was a major motif of the festival because:

(i)   the descent of the Shekinah at the dedication of the Solomon's Temple took place during this feast,[64]

(ii)   the burning lamps represented the Shekinah that was

---

63   Sukkah 5.2 and 5.3 (Mishnah).
64   1 Kgs. 8:2 ff; 2 Chron. 7.

seen as a pillar of fire on their wilderness journey. The wilderness journey when the Shekinah guided them from Egypt to Canaan, was the principal motif of the Festival. According to Jewish tradition, the pillar first appeared to lead Israel from Egypt to Canaan on the 15th Tishri, which was the first day of the feast of Tabernacles.

So when Jesus stood in the shadow of a menorah and proclaimed, *"I am the Light of the world; he who follows Me will not walk in the darkness, but will have the Light of life"* (John 8:12 NASB),[65] He not only affirmed He was the Messiah, but also the Shekinah of God now returned to Israel.

This was the Shekinah that:

- dwelt in the Tabernacle when it was pitched,
- led them and protected them when they journeyed,
- fed them with bread from heaven,
- gave them living water to drink,
- healed all their diseases,
- dispelled the darkness, and guided them to the promised land, and
- resided over the mercy seat in the Temple.

The truth that Jesus was the Shekinah, the visible representation of God, was re-enforced by another one of His declarations at that time: *"Before Abraham was I AM."* At this statement, *"They picked up stones to throw at Him, but Jesus hid Himself and went out of the temple"* (John 8:59). John is repeating and reinforcing the truth, *"The Word became flesh and dwelt among us, and we beheld His glory, the glory as of the only begotten of the Father, full of grace and truth"* (1:14 KJV). John restated in different ways at different points in his gospel that God walked on earth in the person of Jesus.

The brilliant light from the court of women was also intended to represent Messiah, for Isaiah had prophesied of the coming one: *"The people that walked in darkness have seen a great light: they that dwell in the land of the shadow of death, upon them hath*

---

65 cf. John 3:19; 9:5; 12:46.

the light shined" (Isa. 9:2 KJV). As Simeon said when Joseph and Mary brought the Messiah to the Temple for the first time, He was to be *"a light to lighten the Gentiles, and the glory of...Israel"* (Luke 2:32 KJV).

The law required the light of the Sanctuary to be always lit, not that God required light, but it was prophetic of the time when God would kindle for them "the Great Light". The Rabbis would speak of the light with which God wrapped around Himself as a garment, which was reserved under the throne of God for the Messiah.[66] In His days it would shine forth once more. In a Midrash on Lamentations 1:16, the Messiah is designated as the "Enlightener", the words of Daniel 2:22 *"and light dwells with Him"* being applied to Him.

Jesus made a point of finding the newly sighted man later so that He could give him even more light, that is spiritual sight. When Jesus met him again, He asked, *"Do you believe in the Son of God?"* (v. 35). This outcast of Jewish society who was unfamiliar with the Messianic ministry of Jesus responded, *"Who is he, Lord, that I might believe in Him?"* When Jesus replied, *"You have both seen Him and it is He who is talking with you"*, he reacted, *"'Lord, I believe!' And he worshipped Him"* (vv. 36-38). This momentous miracle not only supported His Messianic credentials, and illuminated His latest self-revelatory "I AM" statement, that is: *"I AM the light of the world"* (9:5), but also demonstrated the truth of His claim to be the Son of God (v. 37). It was a work of God on several levels (v. 3).

The timing of the miracle is significant. It took place after the Sanhedrin had declared that they had rejected the Messianic claim of Jesus. So He did not offer it as an attesting sign, nor could the Sanhedrists accept it as such. Nevertheless, Jesus, by performing this and other similar miracles was establishing His claim more and more, compelling His opponents to respond. In the time period between the two encounters with the Messiah, the beggar was interviewed by the Pharisees. They consistently sought to undermine the value of any Messianic miracle and the reputation of the One who performed it. They said, *"We know that this Man is a sinner"* (v. 24), now placing on the Mes-

---

66   Yalk. on Isa. 60.

siah the same stigma that had been placed on the blind beggar; a stigma that had been removed by the miraculous intervention of Jesus. The beggar, newly sighted, could see the inconsistency in their argument. *"Since the world began was it not heard that any man opened the eyes of one that was born blind. If this man were not of God, He could do nothing"* (vv. 32-33 KJV). The Pharisees countered by re-stigmatizing the healed man, *"You were completely born in sins, and are you teaching us?"* (v. 34).

These events finished with a summary by Jesus, *"For judgment I am come into this world, that they which see not might see; and that they which see might be made blind"* (v. 39 KJV). He again branded the Pharisees as "blind leaders of the blind".

The Seventh Significant Miracle in John: Raising a Dead Man

The seventh sign/miracle is the raising of Lazarus (John 11:1-44), whose name means "whom God helps". When Jesus received news that His friend was at the point of death, He not only delayed until Lazarus was dead, but also waited until he had been buried and entombed for four days. When Jesus finally arrived, He voiced the reason for His delay: *"that the Son of God may be glorified through it"* and, *"that you may believe"*. There was a great purpose to His actions. While the Messiah could have returned to Bethany earlier and healed Lazarus prior to his decease, or raised him from the dead on the first or second day, His intention was to demonstrate to the leaders of the Jewish nation, that He was able to raise Lazarus, not just from the grave but from Hades. Because of the framework of Jewish belief at that time, they believed that the soul did not descend into Hades until after three days. Jesus needed to wait until the fourth day to demonstrate fully that His power reached to Hades. This sign would be used to demonstrate to the nation, for the last time, the Messianic credentials of Jesus of Nazareth Furthermore, it was of such a calibre that it would also support His claim to deity, as He said, *"This sickness is…for the glory of God, so that the Son of God may be glorified through it"* (v. 4).

It is this miracle that demonstrated, illustrated, and elucidated, John's inspired assessment of Jesus: *"In Him was life"* (1:4); and,

"He who has the Son has the life; he who does not have the Son of God does not have the life" (1 Jn. 5:12 NASB). Taking a phrase or two from the incident when Jesus forgave the sins of a paralytic before healing him, the Messiah could have asked here: "'whether it is easier, to say, I am the resurrection and the life; or to say, Lazarus come forth? But that you may know that the Son of man is the resurrection and the life, (He said to the deceased) I say unto you, Lazarus come forth!" Then he that was dead exited the tomb while still bound hand and foot with grave clothes.

We will more fully examine the raising of Lazarus later under the heading of "the sign of the prophet Jonah" (chapter 10).

The Eighth Significant Miracle in John: The Miraculous Catch of Fish

The last sign recorded in John's gospel is that which took place at the Sea of Galilee after the resurrection of the Messiah (John 21:1-19). The disciples should have gathered in the mountain region of Galilee (Matt. 28:16), but Peter had initiated a return to their old occupation saying, *"I am going fishing"*. The Greek word used for "I go" is "υπαγω". The word is made up of two elements. The first is "υπω" which can denote secrecy. The second is "αγω" which means "I go". Together it is used to denote the final departure of one who ceases to be another's companion or attendant. Wuest's expanded N.T. translation reads, "Simon Peter says to them, I am going off, breaking my former connections, to my former fishing business." Here is Peter's formal announcement that he was abandoning his preaching mission and going back to his former occupation. The word translated "fishing" is a present infinitive meaning the action is durative, progressive and constant. It refers to the fishing as an occupation. Here then is a crisis. Peter, perhaps still not over his failure when he denied the Messiah, is returning to his old life, and leading the others to join him.

Jesus the Messiah meets the crisis with a double miracle, the first part of which was negative. This team of fisherman worked all night yet their nets were empty. First, the Messiah demonstrated that fishing was not their future. Then, in the morning he stood on the shore incognito and instructed them to cast their nets again, this time on the other side of the boat. They caught 153 fish. This exceptional, miraculous draught of fish bore a remarkable similarity to that which they had experienced three years earlier. Accordingly, they understood the stranger to be the Messiah. On bringing the catch to shore, they were invited to a breakfast of bread and fish that had already been prepared. Thus, on obeying their Lord, their needs were met abundantly.

Some of the detail of the narrative is very illuminating. To emphasize the negative aspect of the miracle, Jesus inquired, *"Children, have you any food?"* (KJV) In the NASB it is, *"Children, you do not have any fish, do you?"* with the extra note, "literally, something eaten with bread". The disciples answered, "No". The inquiry, *"Children, have you any food?"* was usual among the Rabbis of that day, and could mean, "Have you sufficient for one meal?" (in this context, breakfast), or, "I have bread—have you something to go with it?" (Bread is the other symbol of the Melchizadekian blessing[67]). The disciples who had returned to their old occupation did not have enough for one meal. On the other hand, the Messiah had a meal of bread with fish already cooking. And in consequence of the second, positive aspect of the miracle, Jesus invited them to bring the recently caught fish (John 21:10).

John now isolates the name of Peter for his next statement: *"Simon Peter went up and drew the net to land, full of large fish, a hundred and fifty-three; and although there were so many, the net was not torn"* (v. 11 NASB). This is in contrast with what happened at the almost identical miracle when Peter received his call to service (Luke 5:1-11). Then the net broke. But that was when Peter was a fisherman. Since then the Messiah had changed Peter's career: *"...from now on you will be catching men"* (v. 10). While Peter follows his commission as a fisher of men, the net of the gospel will not break.

In this, the last sign in John's gospel, the principle of table fellowship is re-emphasized. They ate with the Lord. In the first sign in John's gospel, table fellowship was prominent. There, He provided wine. Here at the lakeside, He provided bread. Significantly, table fellowship is placed at the heart of the Church's activities, where bread and wine symbolically represent the body

---

67   Gen. 14:18.

and blood of Christ.[68] *"The cup of the blessing that we bless — is it not the fellowship of the blood of the Christ? The bread that we break — is it not the fellowship of the body of the Christ?"* (1 Cor. 10:16, Young's Translation).

The Significance of the Signs in John's Gospel

The signs for the nation before His rejection included turning the water into wine, healing the ruler's son who was at the point of death, healing the impotent man at the pool of Bethesda, and feeding a multitude of people. These indicate that when the Messiah came to them, the nation was a nation in captivity, without freedom and under a hard rule; not only that of Rome, but also that of the Sanhedrin.

(i) They were without blessing and without joy, as in the first sign, they had no wine.

(ii) Nationally, they were at the point of death, as in the second sign.

(iii) The third sign reflects their impotence as a nation, an impotence that was the result of sin, especially that of their leaders.

(iv) Consequently, the people were like sheep without a shepherd, which is the context of the fourth sign.

If they had trusted their Messiah,

(i) they would have had joy "up to the brim", as at the wedding in Cana (John's first sign)

(ii) they would have been restored from the point of death as with the nobleman's son (John's second sign)

(iii) given a new start with a new purpose, as with the paralytic at the pool of Siloam (John's third sign), and

(iv) would have been fed (physically, intellectually and spiritually) by Jesus the Good Shepherd, as was the great crowd (John's fourth sign).

However, the majority of the nation were categorized as "wicked", "evil" and "adulterous". They believed neither the

---

68   Matt. 26:26-28; Mark 14:22-24; Luke 22:19-20.

Scriptures nor their Messiah. They followed the lead of the San-hedrin and rejected the Messianic claims of Jesus. Jesus would give them one last national sign, the sign of the prophet Jonah. The first element of the sign of the prophet Jonah was the raising of Lazarus (the seventh significant miracle in John). This Messianic attesting miracle was not a call to the nation to change their attitude towards Him, but a practical exercise to demonstrate that nothing can melt the hard hearts of those who do not believe the Scriptures, not even someone rising from Hades. The obdurate unbelief of the Jews of Jerusalem, and the Sanhedrin in particular, was stripped bare for all to recognize.

The disciples, on the other hand, were a believing remnant, and saw His glory:

1. At a wedding, in a context of love, when He brought joy by providing wine for the blessing of bride, groom and guests (Sign 1):
    *   It would be a joy, that for the disciples, would be complete and enduring: *"These things I have spoken to you so that My joy may be in you, and that your joy may be made full"* (John 15:11 NASB).
    *   It would be a joy in a context of love: *"Just as the Father has loved Me, I have also loved you; abide in My love"* (v. 9 NASB).
2. On the sea, when He walked on water and calmed the storm, signifying there was no tempest that would be able to engulf them (Sign 5):
    *   His peace is effective in all situations; *"Peace I leave with you; My peace I give to you; not as the world gives do I give to you. Do not let your heart be troubled, nor let it be fearful"* (John 14:27 NASB).
3. At the pool of Siloam, where He opened the eyes of a man born blind (Sign 6) demonstrating that He is the Light of the world:
    *   While they followed Him they would always walk in His light: *"I have come as Light into the world, that everyone who believes in Me may not remain in darkness"* (John 12:46 NASB).

4. At a graveside, where He raised the dead (Sign 7):
    *   He provides resurrection life: *"For as in Adam all die, so also in Christ all will be made alive. But each in his own order: Christ the first fruits, after that those who are Christ's at His coming"* (1 Cor. 15:22-23 NASB).
5. At the lakeside, where they dined on bread and fish (Sign 8):
    *   In the context of the resurrection, they enjoyed fellowship: *"What we have seen and heard we proclaim to you also, that you also may have fellowship with us; and indeed our fellowship is with the Father, and with His Son Jesus Christ"* (1 Jn. 1:3 NASB).

For those who received Him as Messiah, He promised eternal joy, love, peace, light, life and fellowship.

Chapter 7

How Did the Nation's Leaders Investigate His Claims?

As Jesus expected, the news of the leper's healing early in His ministry spread very quickly. The healing of leprosy was a defacto Messianic claim. Jesus, wishing to bring His claim to the attention of the Sanhedrin sent the healed man to the priests to follow the prescribed procedure. In the administration of the law of leprosy, the priest would require answers to three questions.

1. Had he really been a leper? The priest would need either a testimony or a priestly record, or better still, both.
2. Is he now clean? The priests would examine him over a period of seven days to confirm that there was no trace of the disease.
3. What was the agency of his cleansing? Was it the result of an intervention by someone?

The leper of Luke 5 would have the following answers. To the first question—Yes, he had been a leper, indeed a very severe case, as many would testify. As to the second question, after the seven-day period of examination the priest would confirm his healing. Third and last, the leper would confirm that the Messianic claimant, Jesus of Nazareth did it! The healing of the leper required the Sanhedrists to act. Investigating a Messianic claim involved three stages:

(i)   The stage of observation. This first stage required a delegation from the Sanhedrin to visit and observe the ministry of the Messianic claimant, and then return to Jerusalem and report to the authorities. During this stage, the Sanhedrists were not allowed to cross-examine the claimant; only to come to an opinion as to the significance of the Messianic movement. If the movement was significant, they moved to the stage of interrogation. If the movement was considered insignificant then the Sanhedrin would take no further action.

(ii)   The stage of interrogation. If the movement was considered significant, the representatives of the Sanhedrin could question the claimant, check his beliefs, raise objections and receive answers to any concerns they had.

(iii) The stage of decision/declaration. At this stage the Sanhedrin were required to declare whether they upheld or dismissed the Messianic claims of the individual, and give reasons for their decision.

Investigating a Messianic Claim:
Stage 1: The Stage of Observation[69]

The healing of the leper caused such interest that in addition to the delegation coming from Jerusalem for the stage of observation, *"there were Pharisees and teachers of the law sitting by, who had come out of every town of Galilee, Judea, and Jerusalem"* (Luke 5:17). These were in the house where He was—observing, taking note. Five friends, driven by need, came to this house, four of them carrying a fifth who lay on a pallet. Trusting that the young Rabbi, who helped the disadvantaged, could help them, they tried to get admittance to the house, but the crowd was too thick. So climbing to the roof, they made a rough entrance and gently dropped their friend at the feet of the Messiah in silent appeal for His help. Jesus, aware of the delegation from the Sanhedrin and the procedure involved in the stage of observation, took the opportunity presented by the presence of the paralytic

---

69   The three-stage process is as described by Dr. Arnold Fruchtenbaum in his teaching on the life of the Messiah in its Jewish context, available from Ariel Ministries at www.ariel.org.

to demonstrate His Messianic credentials.

The condition of the paralytic man was the result of personal sin, which brought into focus the rabbinical teaching, "the sick is not healed, till all his sins are forgiven him."[70] Deuteronomy lists diseases of body and mind that could cling to those who refuse to honour the Law.[71] From these passages arose the practice of giving up such offenders to a *"cherem"* or curse, that is, giving them up to Satan. For example, a female offender who resisted correction and exhausted all remedies contained in the Law would become *"a curse among her people"* (Num. 5:27). The Messiah remarked on such a one, *"ought not this woman, being a daughter of Abraham, whom Satan has bound—think of it—for eighteen years, be loosed from this bond on the Sabbath?"* (Luke 13:16). The paralytic brought to Jesus was one who had been a stubborn sinner whom Satan had bound!

So Jesus first says, *"Son, be of good cheer; your sins are forgiven you"* (Matt. 9:2). Because it was the stage of observation, the delegation could not question the Messiah but they were making mental notes of objections that would later be raised. So it is recorded, *"And some of the scribes were sitting there and reasoning in their hearts, 'Why does this Man speak blasphemies like this? Who can forgive sins but God alone?'"* (Mark 2:6,7). Their theology, of course, was correct, and confirmed by three of the greatest writers of the T'nach. Daniel said, *"To the Lord our God belong mercy and forgiveness"* (9:9). Moses quoted God's self-revelation: *"The Lord, the Lord God, merciful and gracious, long-suffering and abounding in goodness and truth, keeping mercy for thousands, forgiving iniquity and transgression and sin"* (Ex. 34:6-7). And David couples the healing of the body with the forgiveness of sins: *"Bless the Lord, O my soul, And forget not all His benefits: Who forgives all your iniquities, Who heals all your diseases"* (Ps. 103:2-3). God had never delegated the authority to forgive sins to any other, a truth that was surely included in the statement, *"My glory I will not give to another"* (Isa. 42:8). Although the complaint of the scribes was unspoken, yet the Messiah knew and responded to it: *"But Jesus, knowing their thoughts, said, 'Why do you think evil in your hearts? For which is easier, to say, "Your sins are forgiven you", or to say,*

---

70   Nedarim 41a (Babylonian Talmud).
71   Deut. 28:21-22,27-28,35,59-61.

"Arise and walk?" But that you may know that the Son of Man has power on earth to forgive sins'—then He said to the paralytic, 'Arise, take up your bed, and go to your house.' And he [the paralytic] *arose and departed to his house"* (Matt. 9:4-7). Therefore, this miracle was not only an attesting sign of Messiahship but also implied deity. Of course, there was an immediate effect on the crowd, who marvelled and glorified God. Thus, the great prerogative of deity, the ability to forgive sin—was declared, questioned, validated and recognized, at least by some. The Messiah had further supported His Messianic claim and sent the delegation back to Jerusalem to report a significant Messianic movement. The attesting signs were enough to indicate that the movement deserved further investigation. But the issue that would cause the most difficulty for the Jewish leaders was already visible at this early stage—Jesus' claim to deity! As to His work, He was offering Himself to the nation as the Messiah of God; but as to His person, they would have to appreciate that the Son of God was among them.

On the basis of attesting signs, the Sanhedrin decided to proceed to the stage of interrogation.

Investigating a Messianic Claim: Stage 2: The Stage of Interrogation

Most of the members of the Sanhedrin were either Pharisees or Sadducees. The Pharisees, who were in the majority, considered themselves guardians and cultivators of the "oral law", a body of tradition that had been derived from, and then superimposed on, the T'nach. Therefore, they needed to know the attitude of Jesus to this additional legislation that they obligated the nation to obey—did he accept it or reject it? To understand this issue it is necessary to trace the history of the oral law in order to realize how great an issue it had become at the time of the Messiah.

The History of the Oral Law

The Mishnah declares, "Moses received Torah at Sinai and handed it on to Joshua, Joshua to elders, and elders to prophets. And prophets handed it on to the men of the great assembly…"[72] And so on, down to Hillel and Shammai who were contemporary with the beginning of the Christian era. The Rabbis traced their own system to Ezra and Nehemiah. Their theory was that the Torah, which Moses himself handed down, included the oral law as well as the written law.

The word "Torah" means "teaching" and was understood to be inclusive and was regarded as containing the whole of divine truth, not only that which had already been discerned but also all that in future ages might be brought to light. The explicit was contained in Scripture, the implicit was the further, yet undiscovered meaning, contained in the Torah. The Talmud says, "Even that which an acute disciple shall teach in the presence of his Rabbi has already been said to Moses on Mt. Sinai."[73] Therefore, "Torah" denoted the whole of what, according to Jewish belief, was revealed to man, not merely the written but also the unwritten tradition, the "oral law".

The foundation of the Torah is the Decalogue[74] and the summary of the Decalogue is the Sh'ma: *"Hear, O' Israel: The Lord our God, the Lord is one! You shall love the Lord your God with all your heart, with all your soul, and with all your strength"* (Deut. 6:4-5). According to Rabbinical theory, the T'nach[75] rests on the Pentateuch[76], the Pentateuch rests on the Decalogue and the Sh'ma is the summary of the Decalogue. All Scriptures were to be interpreted in conformity with the Pentateuch. A key figure in the development of the Torah was Ezra. Historically, he is the founder of Jewish legalism.

The historical succession is developed thus: "In ancient times when the Torah was forgotten from Israel, Ezra came up from Babylon and established it. [Some of] it was again forgotten and Hillel the Babylonian came up and established it. Yet again was [some of] it forgotten, and R. Hiyya and his sons

---

72   Abot 1.1 ff (Mishnah).

73   Hagiga I.8.76c (Jerusalem Talmud).

74   The ten commandments.

75   The T'nach (the Old Testament) contains the Law, the Former Prophets, the Latter Prophets, and the Writings. The Law is Genesis to Deuteronomy; the Former Prophets are Joshua to 2 Kings but without Ruth; the Latter Prophets are Isaiah to Malachi, but without Lamentations and Daniel. The Writings are the books that are left—Psalms, Job, Proverbs, Song of Solomon, Ruth, Ecclesiastes, Lamentations, Esther, Daniel, Ezra, Nehemiah, 1 and 2 Chronicles in that order.

76   The five books of Moses.

came up and established it."[77]

Ezra, the founder of Jewish legalism, started the school of Scribes called the Sopherim. He had reasoned that the Babylonian captivity was a judgment of God, the cause of which was broken law. Moses had warned:

> *So watch yourselves, that you do not forget the covenant of the Lord your God which He made with you, and make for yourselves a graven image in the form of anything against which the Lord your God has commanded you. For the Lord your God is a consuming fire, a jealous God. When you become the father of children and children's children and have remained long in the land, and act corruptly, and make an idol in the form of anything, and do that which is evil in the sight of the Lord your God so as to provoke Him to anger, I call heaven and earth to witness against you today, that you will surely perish quickly from the land where you are going over the Jordan to possess it. You shall not live long on it, but will be utterly destroyed. The Lord will scatter you among the peoples, and you will be left few in number among the nations where the Lord drives you* (Deut. 4:23-27 NASB).

Ezra reasoned that to avert a further judgment Israel must obey the law of God. Therefore, Scribes were to examine and to teach the Law of Moses to overcome the lack of knowledge.

However, to the first, laudable aim, they added the seed of something that was to undermine the written Hebrew Scriptures themselves, for to Ezra and the men of the Great Synagogue, was ascribed the ancient saying, "make a fence for the Torah."[78] There are 613 explicit laws in the five books of Moses. These were to be examined and re-enforced. The purpose was to set the bar higher, to make the law stricter, thus preventing even breaking the Mosaic Law inadvertently. It was second generation Sopherim who sought to fulfil that ambition. The principle on which they worked was, a Sopher could disagree with a Sopher but not with the Torah. When they reached a majority agreement then it became binding on all Jews. They used "Pilpul", that is, the logic of deriving another law from the original law. For example, from, *"You shall not boil a young goat in its mother's*

---

77   Sukkah 20a (Babylonian Talmud).
78   Abot. 1.1.I.C (3) (Mishnah).

milk" (Ex. 23:19), came the kosher food laws. Therefore, an observant Jew should not eat meat and dairy products together so there could be no chance of having both the milk of the mother and the meat of the kid seething together in their stomach, thus breaking the Mosaic Law.

In about 30 BC a new school arose—the Tanaim (Repeaters). They said there were too many holes in the fence around the Law. They worked on the principle that a Tana may disagree with a Tana but not with the Sopherim. This meant that the work of the Sopherim could no longer be challenged, so it became as important as the Pentateuch. The work of the Tanaim was still proceeding at the time of the Messiah, which partially explains why the Sanhedrists questioned Him so closely on these matters.

Up to about AD 220 the work of the Sopherim and the Tanaim had been committed to memory and mostly passed on orally. It had never been organized and recorded. But in the third century, Rabbi Judah, the Patriarch, gathered together the work of seven centuries of Jewish Rabbis and teachers and wrote it down—it is called the Mishnah (denoting both teaching and repetition).

The Sopherim and Tanaim claimed great authority for their work. They said, "a more strict rule applies to the teachings of scribes than to the teachings of Torah."[79]

The Conflict Over the Oral Law (1)

So, at the time of the Messiah, the oral law, a binding set of rules which did not prescribe what a person must believe, only what a person must do (sometimes called, "the tradition of the elders") was in its second stage. It was designed to cover every contingency of life and conduct.

The oral law is designated in the New Testament by various forms of words, some of which include the word "tradition", for example, *"tradition of the elders"* (Matt. 15:2; Mark 7:3,5), or, *"your tradition"* (Matt. 15:3,6; Mark 7:9,13), or, the *"tradition of men"* (Mark 7:8). Paul, himself a Pharisee of the Pharisees in his unregenerate state, was a zealous supporter of the oral law and he refers to it as the *"traditions of my fathers"* (Gal. 1:14). Jesus,

79   Sanhedrin 11.3a (Mishnah).

in referring to the oral law in His teaching, used the phrase, *"it was said by them of old time"* (Matt. 5:21,27,43). This is in direct contrast to His references to the Pentateuch where He used the phrase, *"It is written"* (Matt. 4:4,7,10).

The difference between Rabbinism and the teachings of Christ is that Rabbinism, in practice, emphasizes what a man should do, while it is concerned less over what he should believe. Christ prescribes what a man should believe, while his conduct is largely left to his own conscience. Rabbinism insists on works and gives liberty of faith, while Christ insists on faith and gives liberty of works.

The contrast between Jesus' attitude to the Hebrew written scriptures, and His attitude to the oral law is clear in the Gospels. The evidence of the Gospel writers shows that He honoured the Hebrew Scriptures. He quoted the Pentateuch when Satan tempted Him.[80] He often quoted the prophets.[81] He acknowledged Old Testament events such as Noah and the flood,[82] Solomon and the Queen of the south,[83] Jonah and the sea creature and Jonah's preaching at Nineveh,[84] as well as Sodom and Gomorrha.[85] He referred to events from the first and last books of the Hebrew Scriptures—the death of Abel in Genesis and the death of Zacharias in Second Chronicles.[86] If the definition of "Torah" had been confined to the Pentateuch or even to the Hebrew written Scriptures, the Messiah would have been supportive. He said, *"Do not think that I came to destroy the Law or the Prophets. I did not come to destroy but to fulfil"* (Matt. 5:17). But He was unwilling to endorse the oral law, and led opposition to it.

As was intimated earlier, the Pharisees were the champions of the oral law. They thought of themselves as the logical descendents of the Torah movement, begun by Ezra and continued by the *"Hasidim"* (pious/priests) who so valiantly resisted the Hellenization of the Jews. The Hasidim fought, often to

80   Matt. 4:4/Deut. 8:3; Matt. 4:7/Deut. 6:16; Matt. 4:10/Deut. 6:13; 10:20.
81   Matt. 11:10/Mal. 3:1; Isa. 40:3; Matt. 21:13/Isa. 56:7; Jer. 7:11; Matt. 26:31/Zech 13:7.
82   Matt. 24:37 ff.
83   Matt. 12:42.
84   Matt. 12:39 ff.
85   Matt. 10:15; 11:23 ff.
86   Matt. 23:35/Gen. 4:8, 2 Chron. 24:20-22.

the death, every effort of foreign invaders to replace Hebrew culture with Greek culture. The Pharisees, in the same spirit, wished to defend any attack on the traditions for which their fathers had fought and died. As the descendents of the Hasidim, they focused on ritual purity, calling on all households to apply the same standards of purity to the home that the priests observed in the Temple. The Pharisees wanted to establish a kingdom of priests. They were also very concerned with table fellowship (including dietary restrictions), Sabbath observance, tithing and circumcision.

Being guardians of the oral law, they expected Messiah both to commend them and to support their work. They reasoned that the Messiah would surely expect the nation to be a law-abiding people. However, Jesus asserted that Pharisaic legalism was external and though giving the impression that it was designed to please God was, in fact, directed towards man. It was hypocritical, and it negated both faith and love, the two basic ingredients in any relationship with God. Jesus' attitude to the oral law became the focus of conflict and opposition. When He opposed them and their doctrine, they opposed Him and His Messianic claim.

The Scribes and Pharisees, interpreters of the law, used legalism to keep power in their own hands. However, God had never been interested in legalism. Even during Israel's training under the Mosaic Law, the truth was ever, "The just shall live by faith". The Talmud indicates as much. A Talmudic passage[87] states God gave to Moses 613 precepts, but later seers and prophets reduced these to certain basic principles:

1. David reduced them to eleven,[88] *"Lord, who may abide in Your tabernacle? Who may dwell in Your holy hill?*
    (i)   *He who walks uprightly,*
    (ii) *And works righteousness,*
    (iii) *And speaks the truth in his heart;*
    (iv) *He who does not backbite with his tongue,*
    (v)   *Nor does evil to his neighbour,*
    (vi) *Nor does he take up a reproach against his friend;*

---

87   Makkoth 23b-24a.
88   Psalm 15.

(vii) *In whose eyes a vile person is despised,*

(viii) *But he honours those who fear the Lord;*

(ix) *He who swears to his own hurt and does not change;*

(x) *He who does not put out his money at usury,*

(xi) *Nor does he take a bribe against the innocent.*
He who does these things shall never be moved.

2. Isaiah reduced them to six,[89]

    (i) *He who walks righteously and*

    (ii) *speaks uprightly,*

    (iii) *He who despises the gain of oppressions,*

    (iv) *Who gestures with his hands, refusing bribes,*

    (v) *Who stops his ears from hearing of bloodshed,*

    (vi) *And shuts his eyes from seeing evil: He will dwell on high; His place of defense will be the fortress of rocks; Bread will be given him, His water will be sure.*

3. Micah reduced them to three,[90] *He has shown you, O man, what is good; And what does the Lord require of you*

    (i) *But to do justly,*

    (ii) *To love mercy,*

    (iii) *And to walk humbly with your God?*

4. Habakkuk reduced them to one.[91]
"… the just shall live by his faith".

Moreover, when the Messiah quoted the summary of the Law, the Sh'ma, He emphasized love as the key, *"The first of all the commandments is: Hear, O Israel, the Lord our God, the Lord is one. And you shall love the Lord your God with all your heart, with all your soul, with all your mind, and with all your strength. This is the first commandment. And the second, like it, is this: You shall love your neighbour as yourself"* (Mark 12:29-31).

The Conflict Over the Oral Law (2): The Sermon on the Mount

Jesus addressed the teaching of the Pharisees in the Sermon on the Mount. They taught that apart from certain identifiable

---

89   Isa. 33:15-16.
90   Mic. 6:8.
91   Hab. 2:4.

renegades, "all Israelites have a share in the world to come."[92] Therefore, to be born a Jew was sufficient qualification for entry into the coming kingdom. This is why the Jews of Jesus' time would fall back on the defence that they were Abraham's children.[93] The doctrine of the Pharisees was not designed to provide entrance into the kingdom of God, but rather to provide a righteousness that would gain status in the kingdom of God. It was a righteousness that was based on works with no regard to faith. The Sermon on the Mount in Matthew chapters 5, 6 and 7, is the teaching of the Messiah as opposed to the teaching of the Sanhedrists. His main thrust is to encourage true righteousness and reject hypocritical righteousness. The key text is, *"I say to you, that unless your righteousness exceeds the righteousness of the scribes and Pharisees, you will by no means enter the kingdom of heaven"* (Matt. 5:20). His position is clear. It is not enough to be born a Jew. And hypocritical, Pharisaic righteousness does not count. Pursue another kind of righteousness: *"Seek first the kingdom of God and His righteousness, and all these things shall be added to you"* (6:33).

This discourse of the Messiah included examples of the oral law which the Pharisees obeyed with outward, mechanical obedience, which were then contrasted with what is really required — a heart obedience to the true Torah. "It was said by them of old time", or "it hath been said", are the formulae used to introduce the oral law.[94]

Matthew 5:21-26 gives the first comparison: *"you have heard that it was said* [the oral law] *to those of old, 'You shall not murder, and whoever murders will be in danger of the judgment.'"* The Scribes and Pharisees taught that you were only guilty when the act was committed, but Jesus said, *"I say to you that whoever is angry with his brother without a cause shall be in danger of the judgment."* Jesus taught that murder is premeditated and that the sin is committed when the act is planned. God marks the premeditation, therefore Jesus taught, *"Agree with your adversary quickly, while you are on the way with him, lest your adversary deliver you to the judge, the judge hand you over to the officer, and you*

---

92 Sanhedrin 10.1 (Mishnah).
93 cf. Matt. 3:9; John 8:33; Luke 16:24.
94 Matt. 5:21,27,33,38,43 (KJV).

be thrown into prison." In other words, murder in the heart will count against you at the bar of God.

The second comparison is in verses 27-32: *"You have heard that it was said* [the oral law] *to those of old, 'You shall not commit adultery.'"* The Scribes and Pharisees taught that you were only guilty when the act was committed. *"But I say to you that whoever looks at a woman to lust for her has already committed adultery with her in his heart."* Jesus taught that adultery is also premeditated and that the sin was committed when the act was planned. Therefore, deal with lust quickly—metaphorically pluck out the eye and cut off the hand—lest at the bar of God it drags you down to hell. This, of course, is the context of the Messiah's word on divorce, for He continued (first quoting the oral law), *"It was said, 'Whoever sends his wife away, let him give her a certificate of divorce'; but I say to you that everyone who divorces his wife, except for the reason of unchastity, makes her commit adultery; and whoever marries a divorced woman commits adultery"* (Matt. 5:31-32 NASB). The desire to put away one's wife makes him an adulterer. This word of the Messiah was designed to protect a very vulnerable group in Jewish society: women.

Jesus gave three more examples contrasting the righteousness of the oral law with true righteousness. The first of the three is, it is better to obey God from the heart than to outwardly perform vows (vv. 33-37). Second, it is better to have a generous heart when dealing with your fellow man, rather than to follow legalism and seek *"an eye for an eye"* (vv. 38-42). The third example then challenged His hearers to rise yet higher still and follow the example of the Father and *"love your enemies"* (vv. 43-48).

It is proper and pertinent to draw attention to the phrase, *"but I say to you"*. The Messiah chose His words with great care because He was formally announcing what was opposite to the teaching of the Tanaim and therefore was unacceptable to the Pharisees. The oral law, identified in the Bible as *"the tradition of the elders"*, relied on precepts handed on from one generation to another. For example, the Mishnah records the words of R. Joshua: "I have a tradition from Rabban Yohanan b. Zakkai, who heard it from his master, and his master from his master, as a law revealed to Moses at Sinai."[95] But in the case of Jesus He was standing on His own authority as Messiah. Furthermore, in His office as Messiah He was declaring that He had the authority to interpret the law. There is also in this phrasing an element which implied deity, for since He was the giver of the law He therefore needed none other beside Himself to interpret it.

The sermon began with consideration of the inner life. The blessed are the poor in spirit, the ones that mourn, the meek, the merciful, the pure in heart and those that hunger and thirst after righteousness. Chapter 6 of Matthew's gospel returns to the theme of the inner life. For example, the matter of giving alms: *"But when you give to the poor, do not let your left hand know what your right hand is doing, so that your giving will be in secret; and your Father who sees what is done in secret will reward you"* (vv. 3-4 NASB). Then the matter of praying: *"When you pray, go into your room, and when you have shut your door, pray to your Father ... in the secret place"* (v. 6). Then the Messiah turns to the subject of fasting: *"When you fast, anoint your head and wash your face, so that you do not appear to men to be fasting, but to your Father who is in the secret place"* (v. 17).

These were declared in sharp contrast to the hypocritical righteousness of the Pharisees that emphasized outward observances, and hence the warnings. In respect of alms-giving: *"Beware of practicing your righteousness before men to be noticed by them; otherwise you have no reward with your Father who is in heaven. So...do not sound a trumpet before you, as the hypocrites do in the synagogues and in the streets, so that they may be honoured by men. Truly I say to you, they have their reward in full"* (vv. 1-2 NASB). And regarding praying: *"When you pray, you are not to be like the hypocrites; for they love to stand and pray in the synagogues and on the street corners so that they may be seen by men. Truly I say to you, they have their reward in full"* (v. 5). And then with respect to fasting: *"Whenever you fast, do not put on a gloomy face as the hypocrites do, for they neglect their appearance so that they will be noticed by men when they are fasting. Truly I say to you, they have their reward in full"* (v. 16 NASB). The actions of the hypocrites were, according to the Messiah, designed specifically to impress others.

---

95   Eduyyot 8.7 A (Mishnah).

Who are the hypocrites Jesus had in mind? At this time, He identified, by implication, the Scribes and Pharisees, those guardians of the oral law. However, after His official rejection, He named and shamed them: *"Hypocrites! Well did Isaiah prophesy about you, saying: 'These people draw near to Me with their mouth, And honour Me with their lips, But their heart is far from Me'"* (Matt. 15:7,8). Then the seven times repeated, *"Woe to you, scribes and Pharisees, hypocrites!"*[96] There the Lord described them as fools and blind guides. On occasion, He coupled the Pharisees with the Sadducees (16:3); and sometimes with the Herodians (22:18), indicating that they too were hypocrites.

In the same discourse, Jesus taught that Pharisaic righteousness had a wide gate (7:13). As has already been mentioned, they taught that all Israelites have a share in the world to come.[97] Yet, even they would exclude some. "And these are the ones who have no portion in the world to come: He who says, the resurrection of the dead is a teaching which does not derive from the Torah, (2) and the Torah does not come from Heaven; and (3) an Epicurean."[98] This section effectively excluded the Sadducees. A later inclusion seems directed at Jesus, "and those who whisper over a wound and say, *'I will put none of the diseases upon you which I have brought on the Egyptians. For I am the Lord who heals you'* (Ex. 15:26)."[99] Notwithstanding the exceptions, Pharisaic doctrine pronounced almost all Jews "safe"; it had a gate wide enough to take almost every Jew ever born.

Jesus further taught that Pharisaism was a broad road—only outward conformity was required. However, it was a way of works, done publicly, which would only bring the praise of men (Matt. 6:2,16). It was a way that seemed right but led to destruction (7:13). The man that followed the way of the Pharisees would have built his house on sand, a foundation that could not hold it. Paul, the great expositor expressed it thus: *"They being ignorant of God's righteousness, and seeking to establish their own righteousness, have not submitted to the righteousness of God"* (Rom. 10:3).

The Pharisees were also guilty of judging, finding specks

---

96   Matt. 23:13-15,23,25,27,29.
97   Sanhedrin 10.1.A (Mishnah).
98   Sanhedrin 10.1C,D (1),(2),(3) (Mishnah).
99   Sanhedrin 10.1.F (Mishnah).

in the eyes of others, when they had planks in their own eyes (Matt. 7:1 ff). The condemnation pronounced by the Messiah was absolute. They claimed to speak for God but were, in fact, false prophets. They claimed to be the shepherds of Israel but were guilty of decimating the flock like wolves (vv. 15 ff). They pretended to be righteous people, living righteous lives, and bearing righteous fruit, but were, in fact, corrupt trees bearing evil fruit (v. 17). They practiced lawlessness (v. 23), an amazing charge considering that they imposed additional laws on the population. Implicit in this condemnation by the Messiah is the understanding that the imposition of the oral law undermined the Torah.

In contrast, Messianic righteousness had a narrow gate. Only those who accepted Jesus as the Messiah could enter. His followers were on a firm foundation: *"Whoever hears these sayings of Mine, and does them, I will liken him to a wise man who built his house on the rock"* (v. 24).

Messianic righteousness was a narrow way, a way of faith and love.

A way of faith: *"Now if God so clothes the grass of the field, which today is, and tomorrow is thrown into the oven, will He not much more clothe you, O you of little faith? Therefore do not worry, saying, 'What shall we eat?' or 'What shall we drink?' or 'What shall we wear?' For after all these things the Gentiles seek. For your heavenly Father knows that you need all these things. But seek first the kingdom of God and His righteousness, and all these things shall be added to you"* (5:30-33).

And a way of love: *"I say to you, love your enemies, bless those who curse you, do good to those who hate you, and pray for those who spitefully use you and persecute you"* (5:44); *"You shall love the Lord your God with all your heart, with all your soul, and with all your mind. This is the first and great commandment. And the second is like it: You shall love your neighbour as yourself. On these two commandments hang all the Law and the Prophets"* (Matt. 22:37-40).

Stage of Interrogation (Continued)

Returning now to the stage of interrogation, delegates from the Sanhedrin were required to observe the life and ministry of the claimant, and if they thought any action or teaching was questionable they could voice their concerns. When dealing with Jesus of Nazareth, the objections of the Sanhedrists were almost exclusively in the area of the oral law, with questions concerning the Sabbath being the most frequent, since they had given "Sabbath keeping" such a high profile. The fourth command of the decalogue had been expanded by hundreds of additional rules and regulations regarding Sabbath observance to cover nearly all circumstances. For example, the Shabbat section in the Mishnah begins with the detail of those acts of transporting objects from one domain to another, some of which violate the Sabbath. It reads:

1.1   A. [Acts of] transporting objects from one domain to another [which violate] the Sabbath

     (1) are two, which [indeed] are four [for one who is] inside,

     (2) and two which are four [for one who is] outside.

     B. How so?

I.   C. [If on the Sabbath] the beggar stands outside and the householder inside,

     D. [and] the beggar stuck his hand inside and put [a beggar's bowl] into the hand of the householder,

     E. or if he took [something] from inside it and brought it out,

     F. the beggar is liable, the householder is exempt.

II.   G. [If] the householder stuck his hand outside and put [something] into the hand of the beggar,

     H. or if he took [something] from it and brought it inside,

     I. the householder is liable, and the beggar is exempt.

III.   J. [If] the beggar stuck his hand inside, and the householder took [something] from it,

     K. or if [the householder] put something in it and he [the beggar] removed it,

     L. both of them are exempt.

IV.   M. [If] the householder put his hand outside and the beggar took [something] from it,

     N. or if [the beggar] put something into it and [the house-

> holder] brought it back inside,
> O. both of them are exempt.[100]

Jesus condemned this legalism with the words, *"You blind guides, who strain out a gnat and swallow a camel!"* (Matt. 23:24). At the time of Jesus, questions as to what was proper on the Sabbath constantly occupied the minds of the legalists. If a Pharisee was asked, "Why did God make Israel?" it was likely he would have replied, "To honour the Sabbath". In Pharisaism, the Sabbath was personified as the Queen of Israel and the Bride of YHWH.

Each of the synoptics records the incident in which Jesus' hungry disciples plucked the heads of grain to provide sustenance. Since it was on the Sabbath, the investigating Sanhedrists raised it as an issue: *"And when the Pharisees saw it, they said to Him, 'Look, Your disciples are doing what is not lawful to do on the Sabbath!'"* (Matt. 12:2).[101] The Pharisees themselves would not normally walk through a field in case they accidentally uprooted a wayward stalk of grain, thereby becoming guilty of reaping on the Sabbath.

Jesus responded to the question by giving pertinent examples from the T'nach. The first was of David who, when in need, ate of the bread that by law was reserved for the priests. The second was of the priests themselves, whose work substantially increased on the Sabbath because of the higher number of offerings. Neither the actions of David, nor the activities of the priests, received the disapproval of the interpreters of the law. Jesus took the first example from the period of David's rejection, when the officers of a dying dynasty were hounding him. The selection of this event seems to suggest that Jesus knew already that the Sanhedrin would officially reject Him. The second example related to the killing of sacrificial lambs in the Temple as sin offerings, a parallel of some significance. However, the *coup-de-grace* was the claim of the Messiah that, *"The Son of Man is Lord even of the Sabbath"* (Matt. 12:8)[102] — again driving home the point that He was more than Messiah. By this time, it was clear that Jesus was not

---

100   Shabbat 1.1 (Mishnah).
101   cf. Mark 2:24; Luke 6:2.
102   cf. Mark 2:28; Luke 6:5.

going to support the Pharisees by endorsing their oral law.

While the delegation involved in assessing His Messianic credentials were mostly Pharisees, there were others on the Sanhedrin who had an interest in the investigation and decision. They were the Chief Priests—Sadducees who rejected the immortality of the soul, and attributed all human activity to free will and none to providence. Because they did not believe in the resurrection, they expected neither reward nor punishment after death. Therefore, with no restraint placed on their actions by their religious beliefs, they exercised power, not for the good of the nation, but for their own individual gain. Influenced by Greek culture, they cultivated good relations with Rome. They were not interested in any Messiah other than one who would improve their power base in the nation. Jesus rejected their Epicurean lifestyle, their corrupt "business" practices and their defective doctrines. At the beginning of His public ministry, He upset more than just the money-changers' tables in the Temple. He had made it clear that if He were confirmed as Messiah He would "clean up" the Temple, and Annas, Caiaphas and the chief priests could expect to lose their lucrative business. This meant that Jesus would not get their support!

Chapter 8

What was the Decision of the Nation's Leaders?

The third stage of investigating a Messianic claim is the stage of decision and declaration. To repeat, the Pharisaic Sanhedrists decided to reject the Messianic claimant because:

1. He would not protect their position in the nation.
2. He opposed their doctrine.
3. He condemned their lifestyle.

If He were not stopped, they would

1. Lose the adulation of the population.
2. Lose the power they held as interpreters of the oral law.
3. Lose the wealth that their position in the nation provided.

The Sadducean Sanhedrists decided to reject the Messianic claimant because:

1. He opposed their moneymaking ventures.
2. He opposed their doctrine.
3. He condemned their lifestyle

If He were not stopped they would:

1. Lose their political power with Rome
2. Lose their influence over the nation as intermediaries

between Israelites and God.
3. Lose the wealth generated by the monopolies they controlled.

Nevertheless, these reasons for the rejection of the prophet of Nazareth were not for public consumption. The nation's leaders had already begun a rumour-mongering programme but needed some public issue to cause the general population to support their decision. So they brought to Him a very difficult case of healing—significantly a man with an unclean demon, who was both blind and dumb.

Although in the T'nach exorcisms are almost unknown, at the time of the Messiah, Jewish exorcists were having some success. Their pattern of exorcism was to establish communication with the demon, ascertain its name and then addressing it directly, command it in the name of a higher authority to leave. The disciples of the Lord also used this pattern. For example, the seventy returned from their mission saying, *"Lord, even the demons are subject to us in Your name"* (Luke 10:17). Another example, though not typical, is recorded in Acts: *"Then some of the itinerant Jewish exorcists took it upon themselves to call the name of the Lord Jesus over those who had evil spirits, saying, 'We exorcise you by the Jesus whom Paul preaches'"* (Acts 19:13). However, with a dumb demon this communication is difficult, in most cases, impossible. The Lord Himself acknowledged the extra difficulty when the disciples confessed they could not cast out such a demon in the name of the Messiah (Mark 9:17-29). Because, in the Jewish mind, only Messiah would be able to heal these extreme cases, here was a decisive test for Jesus. In this case, because the man was also sightless, the degree of difficulty was increased, yet *"He healed him, so that the blind and mute man both spoke and saw"* (Matt. 12:22). The onlookers immediately understood the significance of this Messianic miracle: *"All the multitudes were amazed and said, 'Could this be the Son of David?'"* (v. 23).

The Sanhedrists were ready with an explanation. Wishing to discredit the sign, they repeated their previously published opinion that Jesus was demon possessed (Matt. 9:34; 10:25). *"This fellow does not cast out demons except by Beelzebub, the ruler of the demons"* (Matt. 12:24). The Sanhedrists accused Jesus of being in league with Satan, and that Satan gave Him His power. Their position, whether they understood it or not, was that the temptation in the wilderness had been successful. They spoke as if Jesus had taken the bribes offered and was now a follower of Satan and a sinner like the rest of Adam's "fallen race". Since Satan had failed to make Jesus the "cast down" one, he was now getting the population to treat Him as such, by this insidious lie. The lie became the accepted opinion of the population. The Sanhedrists never disputed that Jesus performed miracles, but the Talmud reiterates the reason for His rejection—he did it by sorcery, expanding it further by saying He brought magical charms back from Egypt (Egypt was regarded as the special home of magic, an opinion expressed in the Talmud).[103] The Pharisees rejected Jesus as Messiah because He would not endorse the oral law, and support their position in the nation. The Sadducees rejected Jesus as Messiah because He opposed their unholy practices in the Temple, and undermined their position in the nation. But the reason they gave to the nation was not the real reason. They published that Jesus was demon possessed and therefore could not be Israel's Messiah. Thus the climax of the investigation was over the issue of the key attesting sign— the serpent in subjection! They declared that Jesus did not have the serpent in subjection, but the serpent had Jesus in subjection!

---

103   B. Qidd. 49b.; R.T. Herford, <u>Christianity in Talmud and Midrash</u>. (London: Williams & Norgate, 1903) Division 1.A.(8).

Chapter 9

What was the Response of Jesus to their Decision?

There is a point of no return for the hard-hearted. In His dealings with man, God sometimes says, "enough is enough". The judgments at the time of Noah, and then at the tower of Babel, suggest as much. Twice before, in His dealings with Israel, God has pronounced a judgment that affected the whole nation.

(i) The generation of Israelites that rebelled on the journey from Egypt to Canaan under the leadership of Moses suffered such a judgment.

(ii) Then there was the judgment that sent the nation into captivity to Babylon.

(iii) Now there is to be a judgment on the generation that rejected Jesus as Messiah. When they rejected Jesus as Messiah, particularly for such base reasons and in such a way, that generation of Israel was rejected.

When they dismissed Jesus' Messianic claims and when they attributed the good works that He had performed by the Spirit of God, to the power of the Devil (Matt. 12:24), they committed the unpardonable sin. Their lying blasphemy, which still lives today, has no forgiveness (v. 34). Those who attributed the attesting signs to Beelzebub were clearly in the camp of Satan, and Jesus called them a *"brood of vipers"*, words well chosen, for they were true children of the Serpent (John 8:44), and disseminated the lies of the father of lies (vv. 44,55).

Their rejected Messiah had yet one more message for them. When He was asked for yet another attesting sign, He said: *"An evil and adulterous generation craves for a sign; and yet no sign will be given to it but the sign of Jonah the prophet; for just as Jonah was three days and three nights in the belly of the sea-monster, so will the Son of Man be three days and three nights in the heart of the earth"* (Matt. 12:39-40 NASB). This sign, which will be more thoroughly examined in chapter ten, has an extra dimension that the Messiah expressed: *"The men of Nineveh will rise up in the judgment with this generation and condemn it, because they repented at the preaching of Jonah; and indeed a greater than Jonah is here"* (v. 41). *"The queen of the South will rise up in the judgment with this generation and condemn it, for she came from the ends of the earth to hear the wisdom of Solomon; and indeed a greater than Solomon is here"* (v. 42). This suggests that not only have they rejected a prophet greater than Jonah, but they rejected the personified "Wisdom" of God (Prov. 8).

Not only did Jesus prophesy the ultimate fate of that generation of the Jewish nation—the most privileged generation that ever lived, a generation that had the living God walking among them, blessing them and teaching them—but He also prophesied their more immediate fate. He gave it in the form of an illustration, no doubt prompted by the case that caused the final rift: *"When an unclean spirit goes out of a man, he goes through dry places, seeking rest, and finds none. Then he says, 'I will return to my house from which I came.' And when he comes, he finds it empty, swept, and put in order. Then he goes and takes with him seven other spirits more wicked than himself, and they enter and dwell there; and the last state of that man is worse than the first. So shall it also be with this wicked generation"* (vv. 43-45).

The eight woes of Matthew 23 repeat His judgment on the Pharisaic Sanhedrists: *"Serpents, brood of vipers! How can you escape the condemnation of hell? Therefore, indeed, I send you prophets, wise men, and scribes: some of them you will kill and crucify, and some of them you will scourge in your synagogues and persecute from city to city, that on you may come all the righteous blood shed on the earth, from the blood of righteous Abel to the blood of Zechariah, son of Berechiah, whom you murdered between the temple and the altar. Assuredly, I say to you, all these things will come upon this generation"* (23:33-36).

The Rejection of Israel

Replacement theologians hold that God, in Christ, rejected the nation of Israel and permanently replaced them in His purposes with the Church. However, the rejection of Israel by Jesus the Messiah was not a permanent rejection. The Messiah, who always chose His words with great care, spoke of one generation of the nation, "this generation". It is "this generation" of Israel that was rejected, because it was with this generation of Israel that He contended. *"He* [the Son of Man] *must suffer many things and be rejected by this generation"* (Luke 17:25). And His recorded words in Matthew 21:43, *"Therefore I say to you, the kingdom of God will be taken from you and given to a nation bearing the fruits of it"*, were spoken to the leaders of that generation.

It will be that single generation who will stand at the bar of God and be accused of unlawfully rejecting their Messiah: *"The men of Nineveh will rise up in the judgment with this generation and condemn it, because they repented at the preaching of Jonah; and indeed a greater than Jonah is here. The queen of the South will rise up in the judgment with this generation and condemn it, for she came from the ends of the earth to hear the wisdom of Solomon; and indeed a greater than Solomon is here"* Matt. (12:41-42).

Previous generations had rejected the servants of YHWH, but that one generation alone rejected the Son of God. Their own words will condemn them (Matt. 23:31-36). Jesus says as much in His parable of the vinedressers. Their response to the claims of the Lord of the vineyard, presented by the Son and Heir, was: *"This is the heir, come let us kill him"* (Matt 21:38).

The phrase *"this generation"* is used in Matt. 11:16; 12:41-42,45; 23:36; 24:34; Mark 8:12,38; 13:30; Luke 7:31; 11:29 32,50 51; 17:25; 21:32. Qualifying adjectives of "this generation" include "wicked", "evil" and "adulterous". The rejection of this generation by the Son of God was justified!

The supercessionist view that God permanently rejected Israel is incorrect. While it is true that a rejection took place, it was the rejection of a generation. While it would have major implications for future generations, it cannot be used to teach that the Messiah withdrew God's covenantal promises from the nation. As with the wilderness generation at the time of the exodus from Egypt, and as with the generation that went into captivity in Babylon, there is an "until" with this judgment. For the wilderness generation, the "until" lasted 40 years. For the Babylonian captives, the "until" lasted 70 years. Here the "until" is not given a time qualification but a moral dimension. Jesus, referring to His rejection and Israel's subsequent rejection, gives the condition for their restoration: *"O Jerusalem, Jerusalem, the one who kills the prophets and stones those who are sent to her! How often I wanted to gather your children together, as a hen gathers her chicks under her wings, but you were not willing! See! Your house is left to you desolate; for I say to you, you shall see Me no more until you say, 'Blessed is He who comes in the name of the Lord!'"* (Matt. 23:37-39; Luke 13:34-35). Here, He is anticipating a call from a future repentant Israel. Another saying of the Messiah in Matthew supports this. When He spoke to the apostles He anticipated a future restoration of Israel: *"Assuredly I say to you, that in the regeneration, when the Son of Man sits on the throne of His glory, you who have followed Me will also sit on twelve thrones, judging the twelve tribes of Israel"* (Matt. 19:28).

Paul, the great expositor, also believed in the future restoration of Israel when he looked into the future and said, *"All Israel shall be saved"* (Rom. 11:26); and this is the context for that mighty statement: *"The gifts and the calling of God are irrevocable"* (v. 29). Luke, describing the teaching ministry of the resurrected Messiah in Acts, categorizes it as kingdom truth: *"To whom He also presented Himself alive ... being seen by them during forty days and speaking of the things pertaining to the kingdom of God"* (Acts 1:3). Just prior to His ascension they asked, *"Lord, will You at this time restore the kingdom to Israel?"* (v. 6). Jesus did not deny the restoration of Israel, He only informed them that God the Father had not yet published the timetable of it. *"It is not for you to know times or seasons which the Father has put in His own authority"* (v. 7) Paul asked the question, *"I say then, has God cast away His people?"* and answered himself, *"Certainly not!"* (Rom. 11:1).

The Reason for the Rejection of the Generation that Rejected their Messiah

The T'nach gives the reasons for the rejection of the wilderness generation. By examining the narrative of the nation's experience under the ministry of God's first Deliverer, Moses, and by comparing it to the attitude and actions of the nation under the ministry of God's last Deliverer, the Messiah, Jesus, we will be able to identify some of the principles involved in these sweeping judgments of God.

For the wilderness generation, God identified the point of no return to Moses: *"Then the Lord said to Moses: 'How long will these people reject Me? And how long will they not believe Me, with all the signs which I have performed among them?'"* (Num. 14:11). Also, *"All these men who have seen My glory and the signs which I did in Egypt and in the wilderness, and have put Me to the test now these ten times, and have not heeded My voice, they certainly shall not see the land of which I swore to their fathers, nor shall any of those who rejected Me see it"* (vv. 22-23). Notice, how YHWH refers to the rejection of Moses as a rejection of Himself. The rejection of Moses can be identified in the following rebellions.

In the first one listed below, i.e. *"Then they said to Moses, 'Because there were no graves in Egypt, have you taken us away to die in the wilderness.'"* In the second and third, they *"complained against Moses."* In the fourth they, *"contended against Moses"*, and in the ninth and tenth, *"they did not heed Moses."*

The Rabbis list the ten rebellions as follows:

(i)   At the Red Sea: *"Then they said to Moses, 'Because there were no graves in Egypt, have you taken us away to die in the wilderness? Why have you so dealt with us, to bring us up out of Egypt? Is this not the word that we told you in Egypt, saying, "Let us alone that we may serve the Egyptians?" For it would have been better for us to serve the Egyptians than that we should die in the wilderness'"* (Ex. 14:11-12). They were on the threshold of a mighty miracle. If they had only trusted; for the Lord divided the waters of the Red Sea and completed the defeat of Pharaoh.

(ii)   At Marah: *"Now when they came to Marah, they could not drink the waters of Marah, for they were bitter. Therefore the name of it was called Marah. And the people complained against Moses, saying, 'What shall we drink?'"* (Ex. 15:23-24). Again they needed to trust in God! He made the bitter waters sweet and promised that none of the diseases that were common among the Egyptians would affect any Israelite.

(iii)   In the wilderness of Sin: *"Then the whole congregation of the children of Israel complained against Moses and Aaron in the wilderness. And the children of Israel said to them, 'Oh, that we had died by the hand of the Lord in the land of Egypt, when we sat by the pots of meat and when we ate bread to the full! For you have brought us out into this wilderness to kill this whole assembly with hunger'"* (Ex. 16:2-3). This is where YHWH began to rain on them manna from heaven!

(iv)   At Rephidim: *"Then all the congregation of the children of Israel set out on their journey from the Wilderness of Sin, according to the commandment of the Lord, and camped in Rephidim; but there was no water for the people to drink. Therefore the people contended with Moses, and said, 'Give us water, that we may drink.' So Moses said to them, 'Why do you contend with me? Why do you tempt the Lord?' And the people thirsted there for water, and the people complained against Moses, and said, 'Why is it you have brought us up out of Egypt, to kill us and our children and our livestock with thirst?'"* (Ex. 17:1-3). Here, significantly, the Lord provided water from the rock.

(v)   At Horeb, the golden calf revolt: *"And he [Aaron] received the gold from their hand, and he fashioned it with an engraving tool, and made a moulded calf. Then they said, 'This is your god, O Israel, that brought you out of the land of Egypt!'"* (Ex. 32:4). So serious was this rebellion that YHWH implied that the survival of the nation was in the balance. The intercession of Moses, God's Messiah, averted immediate judgment.

(vi) At Tabeerah: The rebellion against the route chosen by
yhwh: *"Now when the people complained, it displeased the
Lord; for the Lord heard it, and His anger was aroused. So
the fire of the Lord burned among them, and consumed some
in the outskirts of the camp"* (Num. 11:1). They survived
once more through the intercession of Moses, although
a great number first died under the judgment of God.

(vii) At the graves of lust: *"Now the mixed multitude who were
among them yielded to intense craving; so the children of Israel also wept again and said: 'Who will give us meat to eat?
We remember the fish which we ate freely in Egypt, the cu-
cumbers, the melons, the leeks, the onions, and the garlic; but
now our whole being is dried up; there is nothing at all except
this manna before our eyes!'"* (Num. 11:4-6). Here yhwh
gave them meat in abundance.

(viii)At Kadesh Barnea: *"So all the congregation lifted up their
voices and cried, and the people wept that night. And all the
children of Israel complained against Moses and Aaron, and
the whole congregation said to them, 'If only we had died in
the land of Egypt! Or if only we had died in this wilderness!
Why has the Lord brought us to this land to fall by the sword,
that our wives and children should become victims? Would it
not be better for us to return to Egypt?' So they said to one
another, 'Let us select a leader and return to Egypt'"* (Num.
14:1-4). The words of this mutiny form the basis of the
judgment of God upon that generation. The rebellious
parents were to die in the wilderness, but the children
would not become victims. yhwh would protect them
and take them into the promised land.

(ix) The rebellion of certain individuals against the commandments of God at the giving of the manna: *"They did
not heed Moses. But some of them left part of it until morning, and it bred worms and stank. And Moses was angry with
them"* (Ex. 16:20).

(x)   And again, the rebellion of certain individuals against the commandments of God at the giving of the manna: *"Now it happened that some of the people went out on the seventh day to gather, but they found none"* (Ex. 16:27).

Even a cursory glance at this will show how the children repeated the sins of the fathers. Here are some examples.

The generation that rejected Jesus repeated the essence of the first rebellion of the wilderness generation. If I may paraphrase the first rebellion to suit the second, "leave us alone that we may serve the Romans. It is better for us to serve the Romans than lose our place and nation."[104]

Despite the rebellion at Marah, God promised, *"none of these diseases"*; providing a wonderful name, "Jehovah Raphah", *"I am the Lord that healeth thee"*. Jesus, *"...healed all who were sick, that it might be fulfilled which was spoken by Isaiah the prophet, saying: He Himself took our infirmities And bore our sicknesses."*[105] Yet they still rejected Him!

When they questioned the beneficence of God at Rephidim, God graciously gave them water from the rock. After they accused Jesus of having a devil, He graciously offered them living water.[106]

Israel, in the wilderness, blasphemed YHWH by assigning the redeeming power that rescued them to an idol. The Israel of Jesus' day blasphemed the Spirit of God, by assigning the miracles performed by the Messiah to the Devil.[107]

Bread of Heaven

Perhaps the most significant rebellion of Israel was the one that took place after the ten listed. It was a revolt that arose from their dislike of the heavenly manna, the food provided by YHWH to sustain them. Their rejection of the bread of heaven can be compared with the rejection of the Messiah, "the Bread of Life". With respect to the wilderness generation, God greatly condemned the rejection of the manna, and because of its high

---

104   cf. Ex. 14:11-12 with John 11:48.
105   cf. Ex. 15:26 with Matt. 8:16-17.
106   cf. Ex. 17:1-3 with John 7:20,37-38.
107   cf. Ex. 32:4 with Matt. 12:24.

significance, did not postpone judgment. The T'nach first gives us the complaint of the rebels: *"...the people spoke against God and against Moses: 'Why have you brought us up out of Egypt to die in the wilderness? For there is no food and no water, and our soul loathes* [detests] *this worthless bread'"* (Num. 21:5). Then follows the description of the reaction of YHWH: *"So the Lord sent fiery serpents among the people, and they bit the people; and many of the people of Israel died"* (v. 6). When that generation rebelled against the bread from heaven, YHWH lifted His protection from the nation, effectively delivering them to Satan, who immediately sent in poisonous serpents to wreak havoc among the rebels! The only antidote to the poison of the snakes was faith in the God who had the serpent in subjection, which faith they could express by looking toward the brass serpent impaled on a pole.

The nation under Caiaphas despised God's provision, Jesus the Messiah, the true bread from heaven. He was *"hated without a cause"* (John 15:25), and He *"endured...hostility from sinners against Himself"* (Heb. 12:3). When Israel rejected God's Son, their Messiah, YHWH lifted his hand of protection (as He had with the wilderness generation) and effectively delivered the nation to Satan. The dogma of the Sanhedrists, like the poison of the serpents in the wilderness, was allowed to course through the veins of the nation. Jesus left Israel to the Pharisees and Sadducees, personnel who mouthed the doctrines of the Serpent and who had the poison of asps under their lips (Rom. 3:13). They would lead the nation to destruction, in the name of patriotism, and in defence of tradition. Those who followed them and their system of righteousness would perish both physically and spiritually. They would be a nation possessed by multiple evils (Matt. 12:45). Those individuals who wished to remain under the protection of God would have to repudiate the decision of Israel's highest court, and receive Jesus of Nazareth as their Messiah, even though the Sanhedrin rejected Him and Rome executed Him. Like those in the wilderness who wished to survive the activity of Satan, they would have to look to the gibbet, where the physical evidence of "the serpent in subjection" was visible. *"As Moses lifted up the serpent in the wilderness, even so must the Son of Man be lifted up, that whoever believes in Him should not perish but have eternal life"* (John 3:14-15).

The suffering Servant of YHWH, in His death, followed a path that was exactly opposite to the path of Lucifer. Lucifer tried to exalt himself, while Jesus humbled Himself. Lucifer rebelled against the will of YHWH, while Jesus Messiah embraced the will of His Father. The results were exactly the opposite too. Lucifer was "cast down", where the Son of God was "lifted up". The rebellion of Satan brought death and suffering whereas the obedience of Messiah brought life and blessing. The Roman gibbet on which He was executed became the symbol of the serpent defeated, for through death He rendered powerless the one who had the power of death, that is, the Devil, and freed those who through fear of death were subject to slavery all their lives (Heb. 2:14-15). God will cast Lucifer down to the lowest depths of the bottomless pit—Jesus will have the highest honour that heaven possesses (Phil. 2:9-11).

The Unpardonable Sin

The national rejection of Jesus as Messiah, coupled with the slander that He was demon possessed, constituted the unpardonable sin. At that point in Israel's history, Jesus withdrew His offer of the immediate Messianic kingdom. He changed the Messianic programme from one coming to two comings. The nation will not now know the reign of their Messiah until Israel's national leaders, in a spirit of humility and repentance, call for His return. The Sanhedrin, the leaders of the nation, were, at the time of the first coming of their Messiah, servants of Mammon (Matt. 6:24), not servants of God, and thus failed to do what was right. Jesus said He would not return until a future generation of the nation calls for Him, and welcomes Him with the appropriate Messianic greeting: *"For I say to you, you shall see Me no more till you say, 'Blessed is He who comes in the name of the Lord!'"* (Matt. 23:39)

The language of the Messiah, after His rejection, was very direct. Facing His opponents, He powerfully described them as a *"generation of vipers"* (Matt. 12:34), *"an evil and adulterous generation"* (v. 39) and a *"wicked generation"* (v. 45). He prophesied their decline and destruction, and said that since they had mouthed the doctrines of the serpent, they would have to justify their words in the judgment chamber of God (vv. 36-37). Jesus warned them, that the men of Nineveh will be called as prosecution witnesses against them, because Nineveh repented and turned to God under the preaching of a prophet while the leaders of this generation would not repent. They did not repent under the ministry of such a man as John, the greatest of the old dispensation prophets, or even more incredibly, under the ministry of God's Son, Jesus Christ.[108] Similarly, testimony from the Queen of the South would also condemn them, because she travelled a great distance to listen to and marvel at the glory and the wisdom of Solomon; but they had rejected a greater than Solomon (Matt. 12:42). Within four decades, the rejection of their Messiah brought the nation to a condition seven times worse than when He began His public ministry (v. 45). While, at the beginning of the Messianic visitation, they were a subjugated nation, within forty years, they were to lose their lives, their privileges and their Temple; and in 100 years, they would lose their land for nearly 2000 years! What a price to pay!

So the offered Messianic kingdom was rejected, the unpardonable sin committed and a judgment pronounced on that generation.

The ministry of the Messiah changed after the unpardonable sin was committed.

Jesus no longer offered the kingdom to the nation, but rather turned His attention to training the Apostles who would be the main strike force of the new religious movement. In the meantime, those individuals who were persuaded of His Messiahship were assured of their personal, spiritual future.

After His rejection by the "special interest" parties in the Sanhedrin, with the counter rejection of that generation of Israel by God, the conflict escalated. Accusation and counter accusation took place. The Pharisees raised issues from the oral law, asking: *"Why do Your disciples transgress the tradition of the elders? For they do not wash their hands when they eat bread"* (Matt. 15:2). As always, the Messiah gave little consequence to their complaint but put His finger on the heart of the conflict

---

108   cf. Matt. 12:41.

between them, *"Why do you also transgress the commandment of God because of your tradition?"* (v. 3). The problem of the Pharisees, here identified by Jesus, was not just that they added to the T'nach, which in itself was unacceptable, but also in certain cases allowed the oral law to negate the T'nach. The matter He used to illustrate the point was the matter of *"Corban"*. To declare your possessions *"Corban"* was to declare they were dedicated to the Lord. If the parents of a Pharisee were in financial need, the obligation on their Pharisee son was to assist them, for the Decalogue commanded, "Honour your mother and your father". However, the tradition of the elders allowed the son to declare his possessions "dedicated to the Lord" (i.e. *Corban*), which then prohibited him from giving them to someone else, including his parents. However, pronouncing his wealth and possessions *"Corban"* did not remove them from his own personal control and he could still use them for his own needs. Therefore declaring one's possessions *"Corban"* had the appearance of being spiritual, when in actual fact it was designed to evade one's proper family obligations. Jesus branded those that took advantage of such loopholes as hypocrites!

The Messiah identified a Scripture that prophesied of this attitude: *"Hypocrites! Well did Isaiah prophesy about you, saying: 'These people draw near to Me with their mouth, And honour Me with their lips, But their heart is far from Me. And in vain they worship Me, Teaching as doctrines the commandments of men'"* (Matt. 15:7-9; Isa. 29:13). Later He said, *"The scribes and the Pharisees sit in Moses' seat...they bind heavy burdens, hard to bear, and lay them on men's shoulders; but they themselves will not move them with one of their fingers. But all their works they do to be seen by men"* (Matt. 23:1-5).

Their hypocritical legalism received the strongest outbursts from the Messiah.

(i) *"...woe to you, scribes and Pharisees, hypocrites! For you shut up the kingdom of heaven against men; for you neither go in yourselves, nor do you allow those who are entering to go in"* (Matt. 23:13).

(ii) *"Woe to you, scribes and Pharisees, hypocrites! For you devour widows' houses, and for a pretence make long prayers. Therefore you will receive greater condemnation"* (v. 14).

(iii) *"Woe to you, scribes and Pharisees, hypocrites! For you travel land and sea to win one proselyte, and when he is won, you make him twice as much a son of hell as yourselves"* (v. 15).

(iv) *"Woe to you, blind guides, who say, 'Whoever swears by the temple, it is nothing; but 'whoever swears by the gold of the temple, he is obliged to perform it.' Fools and blind! For which is greater, the gold or the temple that sanctifies the gold? And, whoever swears by the altar, it is nothing; but whoever swears by the gift that is on it, he is obliged to perform it.' Fools and blind! For which is greater, the gift or the altar that sanctifies the gift?"* (vv. 16-19).

(v) The Messiah put His finger on the weakness of the Pharisaic system: *"Woe to you, scribes and Pharisees, hypocrites! For you pay tithe of mint and anise and cummin, and have neglected the weightier matters of the law: justice and mercy and faith. These you ought to have done, without leaving the others undone"* (v. 23).

(vi) *"Blind guides, who strain out a gnat and swallow a camel! Woe to you, scribes and Pharisees, hypocrites! For you cleanse the outside of the cup and dish, but inside they are full of extortion and self-indulgence. Blind Pharisee, first cleanse the inside of the cup and dish, that the outside of them may be clean also"* (vv. 24-26).

(vii) *"Woe to you, scribes and Pharisees, hypocrites! For you are like whitewashed tombs which indeed appear beautiful outwardly, but inside are full of dead men's bones and all uncleanness. Even so you also outwardly appear righteous to men, but inside you are full of hypocrisy and lawlessness"* (vv. 27-28).

(viii) *"Woe to you, scribes and Pharisees, hypocrites! Because you build the tombs of the prophets and adorn the monuments of the righteous, and say, 'If we had lived in the days of our fathers, we would not have been partakers with them in the blood of the prophets.' Therefore you are witnesses against yourselves that you are sons of those who murdered the prophets. Fill up, then, the measure of your fathers' guilt. Serpents, brood of vipers! How can you escape the condemnation of hell?"* (Matt. 23:29-33).

The eightfold "woe" means there is no reprieve, indeed no hope for these obdurate, blind leaders of the blind: *"blind guides, who strain out a gnat and swallow a camel!"* Jesus, speaking as the coming Judge of all men, detailed the sins of the Messiah-rejecting Scribes and Pharisees, and confirmed their judgment: *"Assuredly, I say to you, all these things will come upon this generation"* (v. 36). What things? *"That on you may come all the righteous blood shed on the earth, from the blood of righteous Abel to the blood of Zechariah, son of Berechiah, whom you murdered between the temple and the altar"* (v. 35). The Hebrew Bible, the T'nach, while containing all 39 books of the Christian Old Testament is ordered differently, and goes from Genesis to Second Chronicles. The example of Abel was taken from the first book of the T'nach (Genesis), and the example of Zacharias was taken from the last book of the T'nach (Second Chronicles). Jesus is saying that the attitude of Israel to God's ministers has been one of constant rebellion. *"O Jerusalem, Jerusalem, the one who kills the prophets and stones those who are sent to her! How often I wanted to gather your children together, as a hen gathers her chicks under her wings, but you were not willing! See! Your house is left to you desolate"* (vv. 37-38). Consequently, He made His return conditional: *"You shall see Me no more till you say, 'Blessed is He who comes in the name of the Lord!'"* (v. 39). *"And Jesus went out and departed from the Temple"* (24:1).

Chapter 10
The Sign of the Prophet Jonah

The sign of the prophet Jonah is the sign of death and resurrection. When it was clear that the leaders of the nation would never accept Him, and that the great majority of the people would follow their leaders' example, Jesus withdrew the offer of the "at hand" kingdom of God. Consequently, the authenticating miracles that He performed to demonstrate that He was their true Messiah ceased. So when He was asked for another attesting sign by the Sanhedrists (Matt. 12:38; Luke 11:16), He responded, *"An evil and adulterous generation seeks after a sign, and no sign will be given to it except the sign of the prophet Jonah"* (Matt. 12:39). By describing them and the nation they led as "evil", He drew a straight line from them to the Evil one whom they were serving. They had charged Him with being manipulated by the Evil one. He countered by declaring that they were the ones who were manipulated by the Evil one. This reversal of the true nature of the opposing protagonists is at the heart of the "light of the world" debate (John 8). In that discussion, Jesus said to them, *"You are of your father the devil, and the desires of your father you want to do. He was a murderer from the beginning, and does not stand in the truth, because there is no truth in him. When he speaks a lie, he speaks from his own resources, for he is a liar and the father of it"* (v. 44). Their response was to repeat their previously formed opinion, *"Do we not say rightly that You are a Samaritan and have a demon?"* (v. 48). When He added the adjective "adulterous" He was describing them in the same way as YHWH described Israel at those times when they left the worship of the one and only true God to follow other lovers, that is other gods. In the case of the generation that rejected Jesus as Messiah, it refers to the fact that they have left the LORD to serve another god, mammon.[109]

His statement, *"no sign will be given...except..."* declared that there would be only one more authenticating sign left for the nation, the sign of the prophet Jonah. He refused to perform any other attesting signs for the nation. There were other miracles—but they were in response to individual need or for the training of the apostles, they were not offered as authenticating signs for his Messianic credentials. Luke added some extra illuminating detail at this turning point in the ministry of the Messiah. He recorded, *"others, testing Him, sought from Him a sign from heaven"* (Luke 11:16). The request of a sign from heaven continued the doctrine that the previous sign was from Hell/Hades, and was a continuation of the strategy of Satan, that the nation should treat Him as demon-possessed, a "cast down one". This is why the Messiah told them that a sign from Hades would be the only further sign they would receive, the sign of the prophet Jonah. Jonah, a man selected by God to warn Nineveh of impending judgment, fled to avoid obeying his divine given orders. He died at sea when swallowed by an oceanic leviathan. Jesus provided a description of the sign: *"For just as Jonah was three days and three nights in the belly of the sea monster, so will the Son of Man be three days and three nights in the heart of the earth"* (Matt. 12:40 NASB). The sign of the prophet Jonah is resurrection from Hades/Sheol.[110] When Jonah died, his body was in the sea creature for three days and three nights, but he himself was in Sheol. Jonah's testimony stated as much. *"I called to the Lord out of my distress, and he answered me; out of the belly of Sheol I cried, and you heard my voice. You cast me into the deep, into the heart of the seas, and the flood surrounded me; all your waves and your billows passed over me. Then I said, 'I am driven away from your sight; how shall I look again upon your holy temple?' The waters closed in over me; the deep surrounded me; weeds were wrapped around my head at the roots of the mountains. I went down to the land whose bars closed upon me forever; yet you brought up my life from the Pit, O Lord my God"* (Jon. 2:2-6 NRSV).

---

109   Luke 16:13-14.

110   These two words are different names applied to the same place, the place of the dead. In Greek it is called Hades, and in Hebrew it is called Sheol.

The Messiah's use of Jonah's experience as a picture of the last sign was so very apt. It worked on several levels, and He referred to it several times in His ministry. In addition, it dovetailed very successfully with the third primary authenticating sign, blood on the ground. The sign of the prophet Jonah will be a miracle mightier than all other miracles, for the Messiah would not only die but also rise again.

The sign of the prophet Jonah had three sections, the death of the Messiah, the burial of the Messiah, and the resurrection of the Messiah. As Paul wrote, *"Christ* [Messiah] *died for our sins according to the Scriptures, and that He was buried, and that He rose again the third day according to the Scriptures"* (1 Cor. 15:3-4 KJV). To ensure that the nation's leaders understood the significance of this last attesting sign, Jesus educated them by instruction and example. He first related to them a true story, and then later performed an extraordinary miracle, John's seventh significant miracle, the raising of Lazarus.

The Rich Man and Lazarus

To prepare the Sanhedrists, those *"servants of Mammon* [wealth]*"*, and *"lovers of money"* (Luke 16:13-14). who had rejected Him (vv. 19-31), He described a certain rich man who had both wealth and position, a condition that the Sanhedrists would have attributed to the blessing of God. The Rabbis taught that wealth was a sign of the favor of God ("whoever the Lord loves He makes rich"). In contrast with the ease and comfort of the rich man, Jesus described the desperate position and condition of a beggar named Lazarus, who must have been daily visible to the wealthy Jew. Lazarus' hopes were not great, just that he might have some crumbs that fell from the rich man's table. In course of time, both men died and went to Hades/Sheol.

This place of the dead had two main compartments, the first part, sometimes called "Abraham's bosom", was reserved for those who died with a true faith in God. This part, in many ways, mirrored heaven. Since animal sacrifice only covered sin, but did not remove it, those who died in faith before the death of the Messiah on the cross, would not go to hell but could not get into heaven, hence the place called Abraham's bosom. The second part of Hades/Sheol was a place for those who had either rebelled against God or failed to respond to the light He offered.

There are three subdivisions of the second part of Hades/Sheol. They are subdivisions of "hell". The first subdivision is the "abyss"; the second subdivision is "Tartarus"; the third subdivision is "Gehenna".

1. The abyss or bottomless pit is a temporary place of confinement for fallen angels (God will imprison Satan there for a thousand years).[111] The demons in the Gadarene Legion *"begged Him that He would not command them to go out into the abyss"* (Luke 8:31).

2. Tartarus is a more permanent place of confinement for fallen angels. *"God did not spare angels when they sinned, but cast them into hell* [Tartarus] *and committed them to pits of darkness, reserved for judgment"* (2 Pet. 2:4). (From here, they go directly to the lake of fire).

3. Gehenna is the place of torment for the wicked. Jesus speaks of it as the destiny of those who rejected Him as Messiah. *"Serpents, brood of vipers! How can you escape the condemnation of hell* [Gehenna]*?"* (Matt. 23:33).

Since they are three subdivisions of Hell, they obviously have many things in common.

Lazarus, whose name means "God helps", went to Abraham's bosom, whereas, contrary to all the teaching of the Pharisees, the rich man went to Hell. The Pharisees taught that all Jews would go to Abraham's bosom, ("all Israelites have a share in the world to come"[112]) but the Messiah related to them the experience of a Jew (he addresses Abraham as "Father" and Abraham responds with "Son"), who is in Hell.

The narrative clearly implied deity because Jesus had knowledge of a conversation between two actual Jews in Hades, after death. He described the torment of the Jewish rich man and the comfort of the beggar named Lazarus. As with Jonah they can speak, remember and pray. The rich man asked Abraham to

111 Rev. 20:3.
112 Sanhedrin 10.1 (Mishnah).

send Lazarus to him with some water to relieve his torment, but Abraham tells him of the gulf between them that is impassable. Unable to obtain any measure of respite, he asked that Lazarus might be despatched from Hades on a mission to his brothers, to persuade them to repent. The wealthy Jew was asking that his family might be given the sign of the prophet Jonah! *"I beg you, father, that you send him to my father's house— for I have five brothers—in order that he may warn them, so that they will not also come to this place of torment"* (Luke 16:27-28 NASB). The torment-ed Jew was unwittingly asking for a Jonah to go to his brothers as Jonah had been sent from Sheol to Nineveh. But his broth-ers had already had that opportunity because a greater than Jonah had preached, *"Repent, for the kingdom of heaven is at hand"* (Matt. 4:17). Abraham replied, *"They have Moses and the Prophets; let them hear them."* Whereupon the rich man said, *"No, Father Abraham: but if someone goes to them from the dead, they will repent"* (Luke 16:30 NASB). He asserted the Bible was not enough—they needed signs and wonders. Abraham responded, *"If they do not listen to Moses and the Prophets, they will not be persuaded even if someone rises from the dead"* (v. 31). If they will not believe and obey the Scriptures, then signs and wonders will make no dif-ference! This was another public warning to the Pharisees.

The Raising of Lazarus

The narrative of the rich man and Lazarus was the first stage of the sign of the prophet Jonah—the stage of education. The second stage would be demonstration through the miracle of raising a man from Hades. The third stage would be participa-tion, when the Messiah himself would return from Hades. Je-sus, at this time, was not reactive but proactive. He was follow-ing a planned timetable. A message came from Bethany to the Messiah that Lazarus, His good friend, was ill (John 11). Jesus said, *"This sickness is not unto death, but for the glory of God, that the Son of God may be glorified through it."* Nevertheless, He not only waited until Lazarus had died, but planned His journey so that when He arrived Lazarus had been dead four days and three nights. When He arrived at the graveside, He indicated that the miracle He was about to perform was the sign for the nation, *"Father, I thank You that You have heard Me. And I know that You always hear Me, but because of the people who are standing by I said it, that they may believe that You sent Me"* (vv. 41-42). He also identified it as a sign of deity, *"Did I not say to you that if you believe, you will see the glory of God?"* (v. 40). So Jesus commanded, *"Lazarus come forth!"* (v. 43). And Lazarus, who had been dead four days, rose from the grave. It was commonly believed by the Jews of Jesus' day that the spirit of the individual did not descend into Hades until after 3 days. Therefore, the raising of Lazarus on the fourth day was a suitable sign for this wicked generation who had asked for a sign from heaven but were given a sign from Hades. It was also the pre-curser for the true sign of the prophet Jonah, in which the Messiah would rise from Hades after three days and three nights.

Because of this final attesting sign, many believed. But the nation's leaders, being fearful that their wealthy, privileged lifestyle could be lost, still plotted to kill Him and to destroy the evidence of the sign: *"The chief priests consulted that they might put Lazarus also to death; because that by reason of him many of the Jews went away, and believed on Jesus"* (John 12:10-11 KJV). Soon after this sign, and immediately after Caiaphas had led the Sanhedrin to agree to the execution of Jesus, the Messiah sent them ten healed lepers, to leave them without excuse! The Messiah had indicated in the relating of the experiences of the rich man and Lazarus, that if they did not believe Moses and the prophets, they would not believe though one was brought back from Hades. By implication, He again says that they did not believe the Scriptures, repeating the essence of an earlier condemnation, *"Do not think that I will accuse you before the Father; the one who accuses you is Moses, in whom you have set your hope. For if you believed Moses, you would believe Me, for he wrote of Me"* (John 4:45-46 NASB).

The condemnation of the nation and its leaders was complete. They did not base their lives on the T'nach, they did not live by faith, and against a wealth of evidence the record of which, if written down, would exhaust all available space on earth (evidence that included having the serpent in subjection, mastery over leprosy, and raising the dead) they rejected God's Son their Messiah. Jesus believed them culpable: *"If I had not done among them the works which no one else did, they would have no sin; but now they have seen and also hated both Me and My Father. But this happened that the word might be fulfilled which is written in their law, 'They hated Me without a cause'"* (John 15:24-25). He described them as a wicked, evil, adulterous generation, who worshipped Mammon. This generation of vipers, rejecting the Word of God, and accepting the word of Satan, spoke with a forked tongue. They followed their father, the Serpent, who is the father of lies. Their web of deceit was never more evident than when events came to their inevitable conclusion; and wicked hands took the holy and innocent Son of God and tried Him for blasphemy and treason.

The Death of the Messiah

The first element in the sign is the death of the Messiah. The Sanhedrists, politically manipulating the Roman justice system, terminated the life of the Messiah at a bloody execution outside Jerusalem. The opponents of Jesus of Nazareth finally silenced the One who had weighed their lives, their work, and their culture, and found them wanting. Using a charge of insurrection, the Chief Priests in their capacity as the main mediators between Israel and Rome, finally obtained the execution order they had been seeking for more than a year. Anticipating the actions of the Sanhedrin and Pilate, Jesus knew that everything was to culminate in the sign of Jonah. Therefore, He began His final journey in the knowledge that His life would soon end. But His eyes were not so much on the cross, as on the ascension: *"Now it came to pass, when the time had come for Him to be received up, that He steadfastly set His face to go to Jerusalem"* (Luke 9:51). The writer to the Hebrews also says He looked for heaven and home: *"Who for the joy that was set before Him endured the cross, despising the shame, and has sat down at the right hand of the throne of God"* (12:2). Jesus tried to prepare the disciples by giving them additional detail of how He would be despatched. *"Behold, we are going up to Jerusalem, and the Son of Man will be betrayed to the chief priests and to the scribes; and they will condemn Him to death, and deliver Him to the Gentiles to mock and to scourge and to crucify. And the third day He will rise again"* (Matt. 20:18-19). It was less than a week before His death that He spoke for the first time of the mode of His execution, crucifixion!

The Trials of Jesus

The Pharisees' rejection of Jesus as Israel's Messiah was mainly the result of His rejection of the oral law. They felt they were fighting a battle, as did the Hasidim before them, against someone who was intent on bringing down the traditions they had sworn to uphold. However, to facilitate their aim and to defeat their enemy, they were prepared to break many of the laws they were committed to defend. These events served to demonstrate that the Pharisaic Sanhedrists were unprincipled hypocrites. When it served their purpose, these so-called defenders and upholders of the oral law trampled over it with impunity. In their ambition to kill the One who branded them as "blind guides", "whitewashed tombs", "sons of hell", "fools", "serpents", "lawless hypocrites" and "brood of vipers", they threw aside any and all respect for the oral law, and rushed to judgment.

The section of the Mishnah called "Sanhedrin" gives the rules for trying capital cases. These were the regulations that governed trials at the time of Christ. Some examples are as follows:

- No arrest was allowed that was effected by a bribe.
- Charges could not originate with the judges.
- Judges were to be humane and kind.
- Judges were not allowed to participate in an arrest.
- There should be no arrests or trials after sunset.
- There were to be no secret trials, only public trials.
- All trials should be in the Temple compound—normally in the chamber of hewn stones.
- No prisoner should be scourged or beaten beforehand.
- There should be no trials before the morning sacrifice.
- All Sanhedrists may argue for acquittal but not all may argue for conviction—at least one must argue for acquittal.
- Witnesses (2 or 3) must agree.
- The accused is not allowed to testify against himself, and cannot be condemned on the basis of his own words alone.

- An accusation of blasphemy is only valid if God's name, YHWH, is pronounced.
- The verdict could not be pronounced at night, only during the day time.
- Voting for the death penalty had to be done by individual count, beginning with the youngest, so that older members could not influence the younger.
- The trial and guilty verdict could not occur at the same time but had to be separated by at least 24 hours.
- There had to be a gap of three days from the guilty verdict to the declaration of the sentence.

To summarize, the laws formulated to govern the trial of those accused of capital crime were humane and considerate. Every precaution was included to ensure a fair and proper trial. Where, when and how a trial was to take place was included in the law. It had to be during the daytime and open to scrutiny, and in a place where the public could observe. Justice had to be done, and had to be seen to be done. A member of the Sanhedrin was required to take up the defence of the accused. Witnesses, whose testimony agreed, were required. The accused would be forbidden to testify against himself—no forced confessions here! There had to be a break between the trial and the verdict, to give time for the proper consideration of the facts of the case. The law timetabled the sentence even further ahead—they built in the delays to allow time for the discovery of new evidence that might aid the case for the defence.

In the trial of Jesus of Nazareth, in their ambition to silence the one authoritative voice that opposed them, they ignored all these regulations.

The defection of Judas had greatly helped the scheming Sanhedrists. With a disciple from the inner circle on board, it would be possible to frame an accusation before Pilate and to have Jesus executed as an insurrectionist. They presented Judas to Pilate as a political witness, using his testimony to support a political charge. On the testimony of Judas, the procurator signed the order for the use of force to arrest Jesus, and he allocated a unit of Roman soldiers for this purpose. Understanding the need for haste during the festival, Pilate also committed himself to be ready early in the morning, to deal with the case.

So the long night, prosecuted by the power of darkness, began with a betrayal (Luke 22:53). Judas went to the garden of Gethsemane, with Roman and Temple guards, to arrest the Messiah (John 18:3). In the garden of Gethsemane, demon-possessed Judas betrayed Jesus with a kiss. Kissing a Rabbi was a sign of discipleship and a sign of homage. Even the mode of betrayal was itself a betrayal, *"Judas, are you betraying the Son of Man with a kiss?"* (Luke 22:48).

The arresting party first took Jesus to Annas. Annas had continued to exert the power of the High Priest even though Rome had deposed him in AD 14. It was in his residence that the first interrogation began. This hearing before Annas, the second hearing before Caiaphas, and the later third hearing before the Sanhedrin, all had the appearance of trials under Jewish law, but were without any of the safeguards of the Mosaic and Mishnaic codes. The first two were held at night, (against the law), and in secret, (against the law), and the accused was physically humiliated (against the law).

In these hearings, special attention was paid to the law of blasphemy.

From the home of Annas, they took Jesus to the palace of Caiaphas, who was son-in-law to Annas and was the current holder of the office of High Priest. At this examination, the testimony of the witnesses did not agree, a situation that in normal circumstances should have ended the trial. Because the witnesses failed to bring convincing evidence, Caiaphas was compelled to use his high office and to unlawfully question Jesus directly, using a formula that compelled a response. The oath, and the question that Caiaphas put to the Messiah, and which demanded an answer was, *"I put You under oath by the living God: Tell us if You are the Christ* [Messiah], *the Son of God!"* (Matt. 26:63). Here Caiaphas put his finger on the significant elements in the matter. Here is the moment in time when the decision by the nation would gain its final, official status. Jesus answered clearly and responded in the affirmative, *"It is as you said. Nevertheless, I say to you, hereafter you will see the Son of Man sitting at the right hand of the Power, and coming on the clouds of heaven"* (v. 64). The whole counsel acted unanimously (and illegally), and proclaimed Him guilty of blasphemy and called for the death sentence. Here, the law-breaking leaders of the nation judicially rejected their Messiah. That all these activities took place at night made them unlawful, and served to demonstrate that these were the servants of the Prince of darkness, and enemies of the Light of the world.

Others in attendance that night, who claimed to be committed to the regulations of the Sanhedrists, ignored the instructions in the law that required them to act humanely, and perpetrated against the prisoner, actions that were high indignities. They abused the Lord of glory with fists, (which under other circumstances would carry a fine of several days' wages); slapped Him across the face, (which could carry a fine of more than six months' wages); and worst of all, in Jewish eyes, spat upon Him, (which could carry a fine of more than a year's wages).

Those who rejected His Messianic claims because He broke the oral law, had no compunction about breaking the same law in at least twenty different instances. The law's requirements regarding the conduct of capital cases were completely ignored, thus proving, *"The heart is deceitful above all things, and desperately wicked"* (Jer. 17:9).

During the humiliation of Jesus, Judas returned the blood money to the Chief Priests, recanted his actions, and then hanged himself. In the morning, as many of the Sanhedrin as could be mustered were gathered together to confirm the verdict and to give the proceedings a look of legality.

The execution of the Messiah: But why crucifixion?
Prior to these events and in the will of God, authority to inflict the death sentence had been removed from the Jewish courts. So it was the Roman justice system that pronounced the guilty verdict and called for the execution of Jesus, *"...that the saying of Jesus might be fulfilled which He spoke, signifying by what death He would die"* (John 18:32). He had prophesied His death on several occasions. First, after Peter properly identified and confessed Him as Messiah: *"You are the Christ, the Son of the living God"* (Matt. 16:16).

"From that time Jesus began to show to His disciples that He must go to Jerusalem, and suffer many things from the elders and chief priests and scribes, and be killed, and be raised the third day" (v. 21).[113] Then again, when they were in Galilee: *"Jesus said to them, The Son of Man is about to be betrayed into the hands of men, and they will kill Him, and the third day He will be raised up"* (Matt. 17:22-23).[114] And then again: *"Behold, we are going up to Jerusalem, and the Son of Man will be betrayed to the chief priests and to the scribes; and they will condemn Him to death, and deliver Him to the Gentiles to mock and to scourge and to crucify. And the third day He will rise again"* (Matt. 20:18-19).[115]

The train of events that had begun in the Garden of Gethsemane moved towards its inevitable conclusion, execution by crucifixion. In fact, Jesus had said God would allow no other way for Him to die as the Saviour of the world. *"As Moses lifted up the serpent in the wilderness, even so must the Son of man be lifted up"* (John 3:14), and again: *"When you lift up the Son of Man, then you will know that I am He"* (John 8:28), and again: *"And I, if I am lifted up from the earth, will draw all peoples to Myself"* (John 12:32).

Jesus would fulfil the prophecy from the Garden of Eden at His execution. As the promised Messiah, He would bruise Satan's head, and the physical manner of His death would demonstrate and symbolize the spiritual defeat of the Adversary. The head of the serpent had to be below the foot of the seed of the woman (Gen. 3:15). Since the serpent was the one "cast down", Jesus, of necessity, had to be the One "lifted up". Therefore, the key phrase is "lifted up". If the execution had remained with the Jews, it would have been one of the four prescribed ways of judicial killing. They were (1) stoning, (2) burning, (3) decapitation, and (4) strangulation.[116] Although those that were stoned to death would be hanged on a tree afterwards, in none of them is the victim "lifted up". In the case of Jesus, under the Jewish judicial system He would have been stoned. Those that are stoned are "cast down". Often, the place of execution was a form of pit. The Mishnah declares the place of stoning has to

---

113   cf. Luke 9:22.
114   cf. Luke 18:33.
115   cf. Luke 24:7.
116   San. 7.1 (B) (Mishnah).

be twice the height of a man.[117] The individual would be stoned from above. To maintain the proper positions of the Messiah and Satan, the Son of man had to be lifted up, and crucifixion, as prophesied in Psalm 22, was the mode of execution that maintained the physical demonstration of the spiritual act.

Roman/Gentile Complicity

The events of the historic night demand further scrutiny. The larger Sanhedrin, having condemned to death their Messiah, then sent a delegation to fulfil the previously arranged appointment with Pilate. However, aiming to obtain a guilty verdict from the Procurator had become much more difficult because their main political witness, Judas, was no longer available. Nevertheless, they pursued the accusation of sedition, but Pilate would have none of it and pronounced Christ innocent of the charge. Nevertheless, the Jews continued to clamor for the death penalty.

Pilate, the personal representative of the Roman Emperor proclaimed Jesus of Nazareth innocent of all charges on six separate occasions, the last time officially from the judgment seat, but the Jewish leadership showed bulldog tenacity in holding firm to their demand for the execution of Jesus. At any stage, the Sanhedrists could have drawn back from their course of action, but they were stubborn and obstinate. They had one more weapon in their armoury—a piece of intelligence that could be used as political blackmail, which they hoped would secure Pilate's compliance. Knowing that the governor was concerned about his position under Caesar, they felt he would be vulnerable to a cleverly worded threat. So they warned him that failure to comply with their demands would result in a report to Rome—a report that would confirm previous rumours of Pilate's complicity in activities to undermine the authority of Caesar. When the threats were voiced, Pilate capitulated and handed the Messiah over for crucifixion. At the same time he gave the order to release Yeshua Barabbas, a man bearing the name "Jesus, Son of the father", who was himself awaiting execution for sedition and murder.

---

117   San. 6.4 (A) (Mishnah).

From the Antonia fortress, where He had been scourged in the parade square, Jesus was brought through the Herodian extensions on the north side of the Temple. Then, just like the lambs for the morning offerings, He was taken through the gate of the lambs, the Tadi gate, before leaving the Temple through the only exit gate on the Eastern wall, the Shushan gate. The red heifer was taken to slaughter through this gate. It was also the gate through which the scapegoat was led. Like the red heifer, Jesus was taken through the Shushan gate to slaughter. Like the scapegoat, Jesus was taken through the Shushan gate, to bear away the sins of the people. They took Him to the place of execution, an ancient holy site named Calvary or Golgotha, the place of a skull.[118] There He was lifted up and crucified. During His hours on the cross, the Messiah fulfilled His own personal responsibility under the Mosaic Law and made provision for His mother by placing her in the care of John.

Other signs that attended the crucifixion included three hours of darkness over the earth, an earthquake, and the rending of the sixty-foot long, four-inch thick, Temple veil from top to bottom.

The Significance of the Death of the Messiah

Going back to the principles laid down in Genesis, spilt blood implies:

1. A substitutionary sacrifice (like the lambs of Abel's flock,[119] or the ram replacing Isaac on the altar),[120]
2. A life taken unjustly (like Abel, the first martyr),[121]
3. A life taken justly (in payment for a crime).[122]

It could be argued that the blood of the Messiah was shed in compliance with these three principles:

1. As a substitutionary sacrifice,

---

118   Matt. 27:33; Mark 15:22; John 19:17.
119   Gen. 4:4.
120   Gen. 22:13.
121   Gen. 4:10.
122   Gen. 9:6.

2. As a life taken unjustly,
3. As payment for a capital crime.

That the death of the Messiah falls into the category of (2) "a life taken unjustly" is self-evident. The judicial killing of Jesus of Nazareth was the murder of the only innocent man who ever lived. He was holy, harmless, undefiled and separate from sinners (Heb. 7:26). Pilate, the only judge that mattered, said, "*I find no fault in this man*" (Luke 23:4; John 19:6).

It was also the payment for (3) capital crime, though not His own. This points to the idea of (1) substitution (one life given instead of another). It is evident that the New Testament emphasis is on this substitutionary aspect of the death of the Messiah. Peter wrote, "*...who Himself bore our sins in His own body on the tree*" (1 Pet. 2:24). Again, "*For Christ also suffered once for sins, the just for the unjust, that He might bring us to God*" (1 Pet. 3:18). Paul wrote, "*For He made Him who knew no sin to be sin for us, that we might become the righteousness of God in Him*" (2 Cor. 5:21). These echo the prophecy of Isaiah, "*He was wounded for our transgressions, He was bruised for our iniquities...All we like sheep have gone astray; We have turned, every one, to his own way; And the Lord has laid on Him the iniquity of us all*" (Isa. 53:5-6).

With Moses, the sacrifice of the Passover lambs, evidenced by the blood applied to the doorways of the homes of the Israelite slaves, was the best illustration of this spiritual principle. Meditation on this momentous event was also the best educator of the nation and Moses commanded them, and future generations, to remember and to celebrate it annually.

Notwithstanding the spiritual principle established at the exodus, the substitutionary nature of the death of the Messiah was not just one life for another but one life instead of all others. This truth is at the heart of the great Adam passage in Romans 5, where Paul wrote that as one man's act of disobedience brought judgment and death to all men, so the act of obedience by One Man brought justification, and removed the death sentence. "*Therefore, as through one man's offence judgment came to all men, resulting in condemnation, even so through one Man's righteous act the free gift came to all men, resulting in justification of life. For as by* one man's disobedience many were made sinners, so also by one Man's obedience many will be made righteous" (vv. 18-19). In his other great Adam passage, he says it even more clearly. "For as in Adam all die, even so in Christ all shall be made alive" (1 Cor. 15:22).

The theological implications of the death of Christ in this manner is normally expressed by such words as "propitiation", "expiation" and "purification".

Historically, there are three stages in the provision of "propitiation."

(i) Because God is holy, His wrath is directed toward sin and must be appeased to spare man from eternal destruction. His wrath was awakened by Adam's transgression.

(ii) God provided the remedy by sending Christ as a sin offering.

(iii) Christ's death assuaged the wrath of God, and satisfied His holiness.

Propitiation is Godward; God is propitiated—His holiness is vindicated and satisfied by the death of Christ. The Greek verb ἱλάσκομαι (propitiation) occurs twice in the New Testament in Luke 18:13 and significantly in Hebrews, "Therefore, in all things He had to be made like His brethren, that He might be a merciful and faithful High Priest in things pertaining to God, to make propitiation for the sins of the people" (2:17). As a noun it appears in John's letters, "And He Himself is the propitiation for our sins, and not for ours only but also for the whole world" (1 Jn. 2:2), and "In this is love, not that we loved God, but that He loved us and sent His Son to be the propitiation for our sins" (1 Jn. 4:10). It appears once again in Paul's writing. "Whom God set forth as a propitiation by His blood, through faith, to demonstrate His righteousness, because in His forbearance God had passed over the sins that were previously committed" (Rom. 3:25).

Expiation is not a word that is found in the New Testament but some translations use it to replace "propitiation" (1 Jn. 4:10 RSV). While the primary meaning of ἱλασμός means "propitiation", it surely contains something of the sense of expiation.

While propitiation is Godward, expiation is manward or rather sinward. It is sin that needs to be expiated. The death of Christ not only propitiated God but also expiated sin, allowing God to *"demonstrate at the present time His righteousness, that He might be just and the justifier of the one who has faith in Jesus"* (Rom. 3:26). The death of Jesus Christ is presented as the ground on which a righteous God can pardon a guilty and sinful race without in any way compromising His righteousness.

The death of Christ provided both blood and water for purification, as John witnessed, *"But one of the soldiers with a spear pierced his side, and forthwith came there out blood and water"* (John 19:34 KJV). John emphasized the miracle of this divine provision with a threefold affirmation:

(i)   *And he who has seen has testified, and*
(ii) *his testimony is true; and*
(iii) *he knows that he is telling the truth, so that you may believe* (John 19:35).

Blood and water are the two cleansing agents under the Mosaic dispensation. The Tabernacle and the Temple, the two centres where the principle of substitution was a daily occurrence, both had two pieces of furniture outside the Holy Place—a laver containing water for cleansing, and an altar which incorporated the shedding of blood, the primary cleansing agent. During the Temple period, the lambs brought for sacrifice were first washed in water, in the Pool of Israel, and then their blood was shed.

Again, the Law required the leper to be purified by the use of blood and water before he could be pronounced ritually "clean". He would bathe in water, and sacrifices would be made, the blood of which would be applied to his right ear, his right thumb and his right big toe (Lev. 14).

Moses ratified the first covenant with blood and water. *"For when Moses had spoken every precept to all the people according to the law, he took the blood of calves and of goats, with water...and sprinkled both the book itself, and all the people"* (Heb. 9:19).

The second covenant was similarly ratified. At His last meal, the celebration of the Passover, the Messiah took the third cup, the cup of blessing and gave it a new significance. He said, *"This cup is the new covenant in my blood, which is shed for you"* (Luke 22:20). The cup that He drank that night was not only wine but mingled wine and water,[123] symbolizing the sacred fluids that would pour from His side at the time of His execution.

While both blood and water are cleansing agents, those major passages that deal with the subject clearly indicate that blood is the primary cleansing agent. The passage that states that the first covenant was ratified by the use of blood and water continues, *"This is the blood of the covenant which God has commanded you. Then likewise he sprinkled with blood both the tabernacle and all the vessels of the ministry. And according to the law almost all things are purified with blood, and without shedding of blood there is no remission"* (Heb. 9:20-22). Jesus, while declaring the cup of mingled wine and water to be the symbol of His sacrifice, identifies the cup as *"the new covenant in My blood"*. When Moses took the water of the Nile and poured it out, it became blood on the ground. Blood is clearly the cleansing agent incorporated in a substitutionary sacrifice. John wrote, *"The blood of Jesus Christ His Son cleanses us from all sin"* (1 Jn. 1:7). It is most clearly stated in the songs of Revelation. *"To Him who loved us and washed us from our sins in His own blood, and has made us kings and priests to His God and Father, to Him be glory and dominion forever and ever. Amen"* (Rev. 1:5-6). An elder described the martyrs of the tribulation: *"These are the ones who come out of the great tribulation, and washed their robes and made them white in the blood of the Lamb"* (Rev. 7:14).

The propitiatory nature of His sacrifice is appropriated, *"through faith in his blood"* (Rom. 3:25 KJV). Individuals are *"justified by His blood"* (Rom. 5:9). Paul wrote, *"We have redemption through His blood"*[124], and *"have been brought near by the blood of Christ"* (Eph. 2:13). Reconciliation and peace come through *"the blood of His cross"* (Col. 1:20). It is the blood of Christ that purges the conscience (Heb. 9:14). It is the blood of Christ that gives access to God (Heb. 10:19). Sanctification comes through the <u>blood of Christ</u> (Heb. 13:12).

123   Pesahim 10.2.I.A (Mishnah).
124   Eph. 1:7; Col. 1:14; 1 Pet. 1:19; Rev. 5:9.

While seemingly subordinate as a cleansing agent, water is not totally overlooked by the New Testament writers. John recorded the symbolic action of the Messiah in the upper room when Jesus washed the feet of the disciples. The mysterious word of explanation related to a secondary cleansing. Simon had protested and refused the foot washing, to which Jesus reacted, *"If I do not wash you, you have no part with Me"* (John 13:8). Simon, missing the point asks for an additional cleansing. Jesus answered, *"'He who is bathed needs only to wash his feet, but is completely clean; and you are clean, but not all of you.' For He knew who would betray Him; therefore He said, 'You are not all clean'"* (vv. 10-11). Clearly, the washing with water was symbolic and was perhaps connected with the requirement that priests in the Temple were not allowed to participate in sacrificial duties unless their feet were washed.

The figurative cleansing nature of water is emphasized by the rite of baptism. Ananias instructed Paul, *"Arise and be baptized, and wash away your sins, calling on the name of the Lord"* (Acts 22:16). Paul referred to the symbolic washing with water in Ephesians, *"Husbands, love your wives, just as Christ also loved the church and gave Himself for her, that He might sanctify and cleanse her with the washing of water by the word, that He might present her to Himself a glorious church, not having spot or wrinkle or any such thing, but that she should be holy and without blemish"* (Eph. 5:25-27). The writer to the Hebrews does not overlook it either. *"Let us draw near with a true heart in full assurance of faith, having our hearts sprinkled from an evil conscience and our bodies washed with pure water"* (Heb. 10:22).

The Burial of the Messiah

Events had reached their predicted end: *"And when they had come to the place called Calvary, there they crucified Him"* (Luke 23:33). It was Joseph of Arimathaea who went to Pilate and obtained the body of Jesus: *"He took it down, wrapped it in linen, and laid it in a tomb that was hewn out of the rock, where no one had ever lain before"* (Luke 23:50-53). Note the change of emphasis, *"they crucified Him"*, but *"he took it down"*, not "Him" but "it", the body of the Messiah. The burial of Jesus was the burial of the body

149

of the Messiah only. Jesus no longer occupied it. He was away somewhere else. He had descended into Hades. Paul wrote, Jesus, *"also first descended into the lower parts of the earth"* (Eph. 4:8-10). And again: *"Do not say in your heart, 'Who will descend into the abyss?' (that is, to bring Christ up from the dead)"* (Rom. 10:6-7). Jesus had prophesied: *"For just as Jonah was three days and three nights in the belly of the sea monster, so will the Son of Man be three days and three nights in the heart of the earth."* Jesus described his destination as *"the heart of the earth"*. Paul, the great expositor, calls it, *"the lower parts of the earth"* and *"the abyss* [the deep]*"*. The garden tomb does not fit these descriptions. The Bible tells of Jonah's experience in these words: *"I went down to the bottoms of the mountains, the earth with its bars closed behind me forever"* and *"You cast me into the deep."* In keeping with this context, an earthquake marked the descent of Christ into Hades (Matt. 27:51).

The descent of the Messiah into Hades is used to emphasize at least two important truths in Scripture: (1) That total victory over Satan would not be accomplished until the kingdom of the dead was under the control of the Lord of life. (2) The second truth suggests the height of the exaltation of the Messiah was in direct contrast with the depth of His humiliation. The Bible states, *"When He ascended on high, He led captivity captive, And gave gifts to men. (Now this, "He ascended" — what does it mean but that He also first descended into the lower parts of the earth? He who descended is also the One who ascended far above all the heavens, that He might fill all things)"* (Eph. 4:8-10). William Kelly writes, "He led those captive who had led the Church captive. We were led captive of the devil, and Christ going up on high passed triumphantly above the power of Satan."[125] Paul also wrote, *"And being found in appearance as a man, He humbled Himself and became obedient to…death, even the death of the cross. Therefore God also has highly exalted Him and given Him the name which is above every name, that at the name of Jesus every knee should bow, of those in heaven, and of those on earth, and of those under the earth, and that every tongue should confess that Jesus Christ is Lord, to the glory of God the Father"* (Phil. 2:8-11).

---

125   William Kelly, Lectures on the Epistle of Paul, the Apostle, to the Ephesians. (Addison: Bible Truth Publishers, 1983) p. 168.

The Resurrection of the Messiah

The sign of Jonah required a resurrection from the grave. Jonah returned from the dead. *"You have brought up my life from the pit, O Lord my God"* (Jon. 2:6). Therefore, Jesus must return from the dead. A Messianic Psalm says, *"For You will not leave my soul in Sheol, nor will You allow Your Holy One to see corruption"* (Ps. 16:10). Peter quoted it in Jerusalem, and applied it to the resurrection of the Messiah (Acts 2:25-28), and had it in his mind's eye when he wrote to the Church at Corinth, *"Christ...rose again the third day according to the scriptures"* (1 Cor. 15:4).

Jesus of Nazareth rose from the dead. A mighty movement in the earth's crust attended the ascent of the Messiah from Hades: *"Behold, there was a great earthquake; for an angel of the Lord descended from heaven, and came and rolled back the stone from the door, and sat on it"* (Matt. 28:2). There were multiples of the sign of the prophet Jonah, i.e. saints returning from Hades (Abraham's bosom): *"graves were opened; and many bodies of the saints who had fallen asleep were raised; and coming out of the graves after His resurrection, they went into the holy city and appeared to many"* (Matt. 27:52-53).

The Sadducees who denied the doctrine of the resurrection must have been much perplexed.[126] In life, Jesus sent them multiples of the leprous "living dead" who had been restored from their pitiable condition. Now in death He sent them multiples of those who had been actually dead but were now living again. Jesus, the Messiah, gave the Sadducees, who knew neither the power of God nor the Scriptures (Matt. 22:29), one unforgettable lesson.

The disciples, during their time with Jesus, struggled to understand the teaching of His personal resurrection. For example Mark tells us: *"He gave them orders not to relate to anyone what they had seen, until the Son of Man rose from the dead. They seized upon that statement, discussing with one another what was the rising from the dead"* (Mark 9:9-10 NASB). But it was clearly important that they should grasp it. On several other occasions He prophesied: *"Behold, we are going up to Jerusalem, and the Son of Man will be betrayed to the chief priests and to the scribes; and they will condemn Him to death, and deliver Him to the Gentiles to mock and to scourge*

---

126   Luke 20:27; Acts 23:6-8.

and to crucify. And the third day He will rise again" (Matt. 20:18-19).[127] In another place He speaks of His resurrection as taking up His life again; *"Therefore My Father loves Me, because I lay down My life that I may take it again. No one takes it from Me, but I lay it down of Myself. I have power to lay it down, and I have power to take it again. This command I have received from My Father"* (John 10:17-18). Here He separated two of the aspects of His rising from the dead: (1) He had the freedom and the ability to return from Hades; (2) He had a charge from the Father to make that choice: *"This command I have received from My Father."* The harmony that is in the Godhead is emphasized here, and those Scriptures that state that God raised Him from the dead[128] are further illuminated by the Messiah's own teaching. The Father gave the Son to death and the Son gave Himself. The Father would raise the Son and the Son would raise Himself.

"But now Christ is risen", for: *"He...presented Himself alive after His suffering by many infallible proofs, being seen by them during forty days and speaking of the things pertaining to the kingdom of God"* (Acts 1:3). There are ten recorded resurrection appearances over a period of almost six weeks.

(i)   To Mary of Magdala (John 20:14 ff).
(ii)   To others of the women (Matt. 28:9-10).
(iii) To Peter on his own (Luke 24:34; 1 Cor. 15:5).
(iv)   To the two on the road to Emmaus (Luke 24:13 ff).
(v)   To a group of disciples when Thomas was absent (Luke 24:36 ff).
(vi)   To the disciples when Thomas was present (John 20:26 ff).
(vii) To the seven disciples by the lake (John 21:1 ff).
(viii) To a company of more than 500, in Galilee (1 Cor. 15:6).
(ix)   To James, the half-brother of the Lord (v. 7).
(x)   To those who witnessed the ascension (Luke 24:50-51; Acts 1:9).

Post-Ascension Appearances
(i)   To Stephen: Acts 7:56.
(ii)   To Paul: Acts 9:3 ff.

127   cf. Matt. 16:21; 17:22-23.
128   Acts 3:15; 4:10; 13:30; 1 Cor. 15:15; Gal. 1:1; Col. 2:12; etc.

The Importance of the Resurrection Appearances to the Disciples

These resurrection appearances were not for the nation, but for the disciples. They confirmed those major truths that have engaged us. Jesus of Nazareth was:

(a) Israel's true Messiah,
(b) and God incarnate.
(c) He is the lifted up One, as physically demonstrated not only by His crucifixion but also by His ascension.
(d) He has the serpent in subjection. His presence at the right hand of power by the throne of God confirms this.
(e) He has the authority to forgive sins, because
(f) He paid the price. The "blood on the ground" was His.

(A) The Truth That Jesus is Israel's Messiah.

To the two on the road to Emmaus, Jesus, as a travelling Rabbi, explained from the T'nach the prophecies of Messiah's suffering, and then connected those prophetic Scriptures to the life of their Master. He explained that the Jesus whom they saw crucified, was in fact *"Messiah the Prince"* of Daniel 9:25, and that the resurrection that they found so difficult to believe, was a part of God's great plan: *"Ought not the Christ* [Messiah] *to have suffered these things and to enter into His glory?"* (Luke 24:26). Later that day, when He visited the gathering of the disciples in Jerusalem, He repeated the discourse; and said to them, *"These are the words which I spoke to you while I was still with you, that all things must be fulfilled which were written in the Law of Moses and the Prophets and the Psalms concerning Me....Thus it is written, and thus it was necessary for the Christ* [Messiah] *to suffer and to rise from the dead the third day"* (vv. 44-46).

(B) The Truth That Jesus is God Incarnate.

The resurrection appearances of Christ are in harmony with the truth of His deity. The ones that John records are consistent with the view that Jesus is the *Memra/Logos*/Word, and as such is divine, the visible representation of God while remaining distinct in Himself. If that is so, then there must be elements in

His appearances and ministry during the six weeks after Easter Sunday that point to Him as the agent of creation, revelation, salvation and the signatory to the New Covenant.

In the first resurrection appearance, the Messiah's words to Mary carry certain implications. He instructed, *"Go to My brethren and say to them, 'I am ascending to My Father and your Father, and to My God and your God'"* (John 20:17). He did not say, "Our Father and our God". Many of the Church fathers called attention to this expression, as expressly designed to differentiate between what God is to Him and to us—His Father essentially, ours not so: our God essentially, His not so: His God only in connection with us: our Father only in connection with Him.

Then again, when He miraculously arrived among the disciples in the locked room where they were hiding, Jesus gave them amazing gifts suited to their immediate needs which are only available from God Himself. First, He granted them peace (John 10:19). It can only be imagined all that was happening in Jerusalem at that time. The disappearance of the body of the Messiah, with all that that implied, must have invigorated an investigation of the Messianic movement with the design of silencing any who remained loyal to Jesus of Nazareth. If they remained in hiding, there was an element of safety; but if they began a public ministry, their lives would be in jeopardy. After Pentecost, some did pay with their life for their loyalty to the Messiah. In such circumstances, peace was the best gift that Jesus could have given them; a peace that did not depend on circumstances; a peace that only the God of peace could provide; a peace that surpassed all understanding (Phil 4:7); a peace that would guard both heart and mind.

Then they were given the Spirit of God. They had a relatively short period to receive instruction from the resurrected Messiah, during which time they had to master facts about His death and resurrection. These were to be the foundation for mighty truths and principles that were, in turn, to be the foundation of Christology for the Church—a set of facts, and a body of truth, which would have to last millennia, for the Messiah would never write a book. He would only pass on the information verbally. Accordingly, they needed the Spirit to lead them into all truth, and to take the things of the Messiah and bring them to mind. The truths that they would disseminate would forever be the life-blood of the Church and essential ingredients in evangelism and teaching. Jesus Messiah *"breathed on them, and said to them, 'Receive the Holy Spirit.'"* He added, *"If you forgive the sins of any, they are forgiven them; if you retain the sins of any, they are retained"* (John 20:22-23). The deity of Christ is the baseline here, since only God can dispense the Spirit of God and can give the authority to bind and loose sins.

The miraculous catch of fish at the Sea of Galilee must have reminded them that all nature belongs to Him. As John remarked: *"All things were made through Him, and without Him nothing was made that was made"* (John 1:3).

(C) The Truth That Jesus is the "Lifted Up" One.

To Mary, in the very place where both Israel and Rome tried to keep Him in the tomb as the "cast down" one, He spoke of a continuing ascent, which commenced with the resurrection but would only cease when He reached the "highest place that heaven affords" — the throne room of God. *"Jesus said to her...'I am ascending to My Father and your Father, and to My God and your God'"* (John 20:17). Mark wrote, *"He was received up into heaven, and sat down at the right hand of God"* (Mark 16:19). The actual ascension, witnessed by the disciples, demonstrated the reality of this truth.

(D) The Truth That Jesus had the Serpent in Subjection

The resurrection of the Messiah, returning from Hades, and appearing in a fashion that demonstrated the future, eternal character of the resurrection bodies of the saints, indicated how complete His victory over Satan was. Never before had the Devil, who had the power of death, lost one from the tomb (Heb. 2:14) There were those who had been raised from the dead before, but they always returned to the grave. But, this time is different. The new body is incorruptible, immortal, glorious, and spiritual (1 Cor. 15:43-44,53). It is not subject to natural laws—it can pass through walls, travel at the speed of thought, and clothe itself. In fact, although flesh and bone, it has the Spirit as its engine, not the flesh. "Walking in the Spirit" is a true description of the activity of the resurrection body. The Messiah "abolished death" (2 Tim. 1:10). Such was His mighty victory over Satan.

(E) The Truth That Jesus Can Forgive Sins.

He exercised this prerogative of deity when He included them in the ministry of salvation, *"If you forgive the sins of any, their sins have been forgiven them; if you retain the sins of any, they have been retained"* (John 20:23 NASB). While He does not abdicate His divine position as the forgiver of sins, He allows the Apostolic band to be associated with Him in this vital ministry. The main purpose in this delegated authority is to lay the ground rules for the dispensing of spiritual blessing in the new entity, the Church.

The Importance of the Resurrection/Ascension of Christ.

The Messiahship of Jesus of Nazareth rests on His resurrection/ascension. When they asked Him for another attesting sign, He promised the sign of the prophet Jonah, the sign of death and resurrection. If He did not rise from the dead, then the Jewish leadership would have been right in refusing to recognize Him as Messiah.

The Divinity of the Messiah rests on His resurrection/ascension. Jesus Christ was: *"declared to be the Son of God with power according to the Spirit of holiness, by the resurrection from the dead"* (Rom. 1:4). As previously mentioned, not only did He have power over His own life, but He was able to permit His enemies to participate in His death knowing He could take His life up again. He said, *"Destroy this temple, and in three days I will raise it up...but He was speaking of the temple of His body"* (John 2:19-21 NASB). This power over life and death is divine!

The Sovereignty of the Messiah rests on His resurrection/ascension. Paul wrote: *"For to this end Christ died and rose and lived again, that He might be Lord of both the dead and the living"* (Rom. 14:9).

The Present Intercessionary Ministry of the Messiah rests on His resurrection/ascension: *"It is Christ who...is...risen, who is even at the right hand of God, who also makes intercession for us"*

(Rom. 8:34).

Our Justification rests on His resurrection/ascension: *"Jesus our Lord...who was delivered up because of our offences, and was raised because of our justification"* (Rom. 4:25).

Our Regeneration rests on His resurrection/ascension: *"Blessed be the God and Father of our Lord Jesus Christ, who according to His abundant mercy has begotten us again to a living hope through the resurrection of Jesus Christ from the dead"* (1 Pet. 1:3).

Our Present Life rests on His resurrection/ascension: *"...just as Christ was raised from the dead by the glory of the Father, even so we also should walk in newness of life"* (Rom. 6:4).

Our Resurrection rests on His resurrection/ascension: *"But now Christ is risen from the dead, and has become the firstfruits of those who have fallen asleep ... For as in Adam all die, even so in Christ all shall be made alive. But each one in his own order: Christ the firstfruits, afterward those who are Christ's at His coming"* (1 Cor. 15:20-23).

The resurrection of Christ is essential to the whole doctrine of redemption: *"But if there is no resurrection of the dead, then Christ is not risen. And if Christ is not risen, then our preaching is empty and your faith is also empty ... And if Christ is not risen, your faith is futile; you are still in your sins!"* (1 Cor. 15:13-17).

Chapter 11

A Final Summary

Let us ask our questions again, and summarize our answers.

Did the Jewish nation have any expectation of a Messiah at the beginning of the Christian era? Some historical indicators suggest there was such anticipation, at least among some of the population of Israel. The Baptist's ministry mightily increased this anticipation.

Did Jesus claim to be the promised Messiah? Yes! His claim to be the fulfilment of the Messianic promise of Isaiah 61 would be enough, but repeatedly through His ministry, He called for people to accept Him as such, with dire consequences if they did not. He said, *"Ye shall die in your sins: for if ye believe not that I am He, ye shall die in your sins"* (John 8:24).[129]

Did Jesus of Nazareth claim to be God incarnate? Yes He did, both obliquely and directly. This claim was the most difficult for the Sanhedrists to evaluate. Rejection of this claim allowed them to justify to the public their complicity in the execution of Jesus.

What evidence was the Messiah expected to provide to support His claim? The attesting signs were familiar to the students of the T'nach arising from those identified as attesting signs for the great Jewish prophet and deliverer Moses.

Did Jesus of Nazareth provide that evidence to support His Messianic claim? Yes! His ministry is peppered with attesting miracles, especially the healing of leprosy (in one recorded instance ten lepers healed at the same time), and the casting out of demons in large numbers. The quantity and quality of healings

---

129   cf. John 8:28; 13:19; 18:5-6,8.

and exorcisms testified that heaven was in harmony with the miraculous ministry of Christ. *"The works which the Father hath given me to finish—the very works that I do—bear witness of Me"* (John 5:36).

How did the nation's leaders investigate His claims? They followed the accepted procedures. First investigating, then interrogating and finally deciding. So striking was the ministry of Jesus that the Sanhedrists were compelled to spend many man-hours checking, debating and evaluating the claim of the prophet from Nazareth.

What was the decision of the nation's leaders? How did the Jews react to His claims? The leaders rejected them, and led the bulk of the population to reject them also. The Scribes and Pharisees rejected the Messiah because He exposed their hypocrisy, and opposed both their commitment to the oral law, and their position as interpreters of the law. The Sadducees rejected Him because He opposed both their doctrine and their hypocrisy. He opposed their doctrine because it was weak and limited, being based on the Pentateuch alone. He exposed the hypocrisy of the many Sadducean priests who gave lip service to holiness by following the rules of purity imposed by the Pentateuch, while being corrupt, running the Temple as their own personal moneymaking monopoly. The rejection of the Messiah was summarized, *"light has come into the world, and men loved darkness rather than light, because their deeds were evil"* (3:19).

What was the response of Jesus to their decision? He rejected that generation of Israel. The nation contemporary with the coming of their Messiah, as a unit, lost the opportunity to be a part of the Messianic kingdom. He postponed the Messianic kingdom until a repentant Jewish nation would call for His return. Individual Jews could repent and be saved but the nation's leaders had wasted this national opportunity.

What happened next? The sign of the prophet Jonah. The first part of the sign was the death of the Messiah (blood on the ground). The second part was His burial, His descent into Hades. The third part of the sign was His resurrection. The highest exaltation followed the humiliation of Messiah.

And then? From the throne of God, the Christ of God sent the

Spirit of God, to equip and guide the Church. The commissioned apostles of the Messiah went everywhere preaching His gospel, a gospel of a crucified, resurrected and exalted Messiah, they too providing attesting and authenticating signs.

Bibliography

Edersheim, Alfred. The Life and Time of Jesus the Messiah. Peabody: Hendrickson Publishers Inc., 2000.

Garrard, Alec. The Splendour of the Temple. Grand Rapids: Kregel Publications, 1997.

Herford, R.T. Christianity in Talmud and Midrash. London: Williams & Norgate, 1903.

Keil, C.F. & Delitzsch, F., Commentary on the Old Testament, Electronic Edition. Peabody: Hendrickson Publishers Inc., 2002.

Kelly, William. Lectures on the Epistle of Paul, the Apostle, to the Ephesians. Addison: Bible Truth Publishers, 1983.

Kosofsky, Scott-Martin. The Book of Customs, A Complete Handbook for the Jewish Year. San Francisco: Harper, 2004.

Lightfoot, John. Commentary on the New Testament from the Talmud and Hebraica. Peabody: Hendrickson Publishers Inc., 2003.

Neusner, Jacob. The Mishnah: A New Translation. London: Yale University Press, 1988.

The Aramaic Bible—The Targums. Translated with introductions, apparatus and notes under project director Martin MᶜNamara. Edinburgh: T & T Clark Ltd., 1987-1992.

The Babylonian Talmud. Trans. Rabbi Dr. I. Epstein. Brooklyn: Soncino Press, 1938.

The Works of Josephus. Trans. William Whiston. Peabody: Hendrickson Publishers Inc., 2001.

The Treasury of Scripture Knowledge: Five Hundred Thousand Scripture References and Parallel Passages. Oak Harbor: Logos Research Systems Inc., 1995.

BEHOLD THE SAVIOUR

CONTEMPLATING THE VAST WORTH OF THE SAVIOUR

It was refreshing and encouraging to read a book, that did not focus on man's needs or a "how to" method for success. *Behold the Saviour* focuses on the Lord Jesus: His Godhood, human goodness and glories as revealed in the multi-faceted presentation of Holy Scriptures. For when we behold Him in His glory we are *"changed into the same image from glory to glory, even as by the Spirit of the Lord"* (2 Cor. 3:18).

> —Anonymous Pre-Publication Reviewer
> (to Christ be the glory!)

Charles Haddon Spurgeon once said, "The more you know about Christ, the less you will be satisfied with superficial views of Him." The more we know of Christ, the more we will love and experience Him. This study has refreshed my soul. In the long hours of contemplating the vast worth that the Father attaches to every aspect of the Saviour's life, I have been encouraged to love Him more. If you're feeling a bit dry or spiritually despondent, *Behold the Saviour* afresh — and may the Holy Spirit ignite your passion for Christ and invigorate your ministry for Him.   —Warren Henderson

---

Binding: Paper

Size: 5.5" X 8.5"

Page Count: 176 pages

Item #: B-7272

ISBN : 1-897117-26-4

Genre: Christian Living

Warren Henderson

An aerospace engineer, who now serves the Lord with his wife Brenda in "full time" ministry. They are commended by Believers Bible Chapel in Rockford, Illinois. Warren is an itinerant Bible teacher and is involved in writing, evangelism, and church planting

---

 GOSPEL FOLIO PRESS

I WILL PUBLISH THE NAME OF THE LORD

304 Killaly St. West | Port Colborne | ON | L3K 6A6 | Canada | 1 800 952 2382 | E-mail: info@gospelfolio.com | www.gospelfolio.com

PHILIPPIANS
THE MIND OF CHRIST

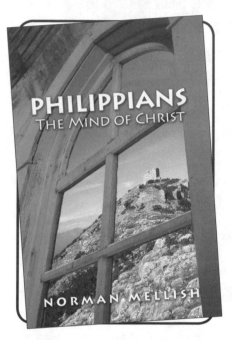

In recent times Norman Mellish has had a desire to put into writing some of the precious things that the Lord has revealed to him. Much of what he has gleaned is from the faithful ministry of good men who sought to instruct him in divine things, and he is very thankful for those who have left a written ministry. He feels that the truth of Philippians is sadly neglected in practice as we move one with another, and if any book would be a means of glorifying the Lord we love, it is by putting the truth of Philippians into practice. It is the highest truth in the New Testament, that is to be like Christ and to be conformed to His image. He trusts that the Lord will use it to bring honour to Him.

Norman Mellish

Although born into an ungodly home, he attended Sunday school. However, as a young boy he forsook the right way of the Lord. It wasn't until he was 15 year old, when God confronted him with the thoughts of eternity, that he returned to the Gospel Hall, heard the gospel of the grace of God, and trusted the Lord Jesus as his Saviour. As a young man the Lord exercised him to preach the gospel, as a result he started gospel tent meetings in the city of Manchester UK at the age of 28. After 5 years of tent work in the city, the Lord led him into full time ministry. In 1968 he was commended by the Wythenshawe assembly. He has been to the British Isles, North America, Brazil, Australia, and various parts of Europe to preach the gospel and minister the truth of God to those who love God's name.

Binding: Paper

Size: 5.5" X 8.5"

Page Count: 228 pages

Item #: B- 7213

ISBN : 1-897117-21-3

Genre: Commentary

GOSPEL FOLIO PRESS
I WILL PUBLISH THE NAME OF THE LORD

304 Killaly St. West | Port Colborne | ON | L3K 6A6 | Canada | 1 800 952 2382 | E-mail: info@gospelfolio.com | www.gospelfolio.com

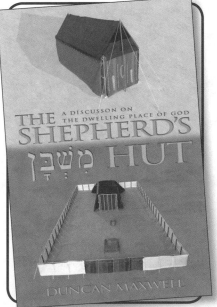

KNOW THE BOOK

| Bible Survey At A Glance

KNOW THE BOOK | Bible Survey At A Glance

E. A. Johnston

Know The Book: Bible Survey At A Glance is a survey of each book of the Bible. At a glance the reader can grasp the central truths and content of each book. It is a helpful extra tool that can assist the reader:

- Prepare Messages
- Aid in Bible Studies
- Teach Sunday School Classes

Know The Book: Bible Survey At A Glance will help you understand the history and time period of each book of the Bible at a glance. Difficult words (places and names) are pronounced for you. A practical application is presented with each book for today's Christian believer.

It is our desire that this research tool will enable the reader to be more knowledgeable, be more interesting, and be more effective in teaching, preaching and in the study of the Word of God. May God bless you as you handle His Holy Word!

Binding: **Paper**

Size: **6.0" X 9.0 "**

Page Count: **148 pages**

Item #: **B-7337**

ISBN : **1-897117-33-7**

Genre: **Bible Study**

Dr. E. A. Johnston

He is a fellow of the Stephen Olford Institute for Biblical Preaching, and is actively involved in Bible teaching and disciple making. He is the author of No Turning Back, Realities of Revival, and A Heart Awake, The Authorized Biography of J. Sidlow Baxter. He lives in Memphis, TN.

GOSPEL FOLIO PRESS

I WILL PUBLISH THE NAME OF THE LORD

304 Killaly St. West | Port Colborne | ON | L3K 6A6 | Canada | 1 800 952 2382 | E-mail: info@gospelfolio.com | www.gospelfolio.com